The West Country

Books by W.A. Poucher
available from Constable

Scotland
Wales
The Lake District
The Highlands of Scotland
The Alps
*The Yorkshire Dales
 and the Peak District*
The magic of Skye
The Scottish Peaks
The Peak and Pennines
The Lakeland Peaks
The Welsh Peaks

Other books now out of print

The backbone of England
Climbing with a camera
Escape to the hills
A camera in the Cairngorms
Scotland through the lens
Highland holiday
The North Western Highlands
Lakeland scrapbook
Lakeland through the lens
Lakeland holiday
Lakeland journey
Over lakeland fells
Wanderings in Wales
Snowdonia through the lens
Snowdon holiday
Peak panorama
The Surrey hills
The magic of the Dolomites
West country journey
Journey into Ireland

Dartmoor ponies near Dunnabridge

(overleaf)

These sturdy little beasts are now facing extinction, partly because they have largely outlived their usefulness as working animals, and partly because they have interbred.

THE WEST COUNTRY
W. A. Poucher

Constable London

First published in Great Britain 1984
by Constable and Company Ltd
10 Orange Street London WC2H 7EG
Copyright © 1984 by W.A. Poucher
Reprinted 1987
ISBN 0 09 465940 0
Text filmset by Servis Filmsetting Ltd, Manchester
printed and bound in Japan by
Dai Nippon Company, Tokyo

The Photographs

4/5	Dartmoor ponies near Dunnabridge (frontispiece)
12/13	Moor and valley
14/15	Two Tors near Okehampton
16/17	View from Yes Tor
18/19	Vixen Tor
20/21	Vixen Tor from the south
22/23	Standing stones at Merrivale
24/25	Two Bridges
26/27	Dartmeet
28/29	The old clapper bridge at Dartmeet
30/31	Rippon Tor
32/33	Haytor and Saddle Tor
34/35	The west face of Haytor
36/37	Climbing Haytor
38/39	Haytor rocks
40–43	Bonehill Rocks
44	Hound Tor
46/47	Hound Tor in autumn
48/49	Hound Tor's prehistoric past
50/51	Bowerman's Nose
52/53	Grimspound
54/55	Bennett's Cross, near Grimspound
56/57	Postbridge
58/59	Wild ponies
60/61	The Devon coast
62/65	The Cornish coast
66/67	Teignmouth
68/69	Shaldon
70/71	Hope Cove
72/73	Thurlestone
74/75	East Looe
76/77	Polperro
78/79	Artists' paradise
80/81	Polperro harbour
82	Boat at anchor
84/85	Carlyon Bay
86/87	Charlestown
88/89	Roche
90/91	The ruined chapel
92–95	Mevagissey
96	Still waters
98/99	The Lizard
100/101	Sun-drenched cliffs

102/103 A Cornish hamlet
104/105 Sandy bay near Kynance Cove
106/107 Kynance Cove
108/109 Rough seas
110/111 Mullion Cove and harbour
112/113 Sunset over Mullion Cove
114/115 St Michael's Mount
116/117 Newlyn
118/119 Mousehole harbour
120/121 Lamorna Cove and granite quarry
122/123 Porthcurno beach
124/125 The Logan Rock in daylight
126/127 The Logan Rock in the evening
128/129 Land's End
130/131 Land's End Hotel
132/133 The Armed Knight Rock
134/135 The first and last house in England
136/137 Coastguard lookout
138/139 Fishermen at St Ives
140/141 The bay of St Ives
142/143 The town beach, St Ives
144/145 Godrevy lighthouse
146 Natural bridge
148–151 Hell's Mouth
152/153 Fistral Bay
154/155 Newquay harbour
156/157 Bedruthan Steps
158/159 Low tide at Bedruthan Steps
160/161 Resting above Bedruthan Steps
162/163 Padstow harbour
164/165 Wadebridge
166/167 King Domiert's Stone
168/169 Trevethy Quoit
170/171 The Hurlers
172/173 Trevethy Stone
174 The Cheesewring
176/177 Bodmin Moor
178/179 Jamaica Inn, Bolventor
180 Tintagel
182/183 King Arthur's castle
184/185 Boscastle
186/187 Looking out to the Atlantic
188/189 Lobster pots at Bude
190 Bude Canal
192/193 The view from Hartland Quay
194/195 Clovelly

196 Clovelly harbour
198/199 Bideford bridge
200/201 The Valley of the Rocks
202/203 Wells Cathedral

Preface

The scenery of Britain's West Country has always been famous for the variety of its beauty. Its chief charm lies, of course, in the coastline, where precipitous headlands confront the sea, often with quaint fishing villages or secluded sandy coves at their feet; but there is also the rugged hinterland whose lonely moors, dotted with weird granite tors, boast some of the most noteworthy stone antiquities to be found in Britain.

The term 'West Country' is often used to include Dorset and Somerset, but this book concentrates on Devon and Cornwall only – that south-westernmost peninsula of England thrusting out towards the Atlantic. The pictures were taken over many years, during which I was chiefly climbing and photographing the wilder and more mountainous parts of the British Isles. When I came to study cliff scenery and seascapes, I discovered that they present the photographer with special problems. Whereas wind is desirable when photographing rocks and sea, because it induces fine water-play, calm weather is necessary when photographing picturesque harbours, so as to capture reflections of mast and hull at their best. But, as I found to my cost after many a wasted journey, fine windless days are useless if one arrives at the harbour *when the tide is out*!

The Cornish seaboard is magnificent throughout its length, offering innumerable and varied subjects for the camera. Devon's southern coastline, on the other hand, is beautiful in a more conventional seaside manner, but offers little that is really striking. However, the sublime beauty of Dartmoor, especially in wild weather, more than compensates the photographer for any lack of grandeur on the coast. It is not only the lonely tors that make good pictures, but also the little valleys – many richly wooded, with streams winding through them – that intersect the moors.

The pictures in this book, nearly 100 in all, begin with the tors dominating the sombre Dartmoor landscape and then follow Devon's southern coastline around, through Cornwall to Land's End. This way the sun will be at its most favourable angle both for viewing and for photography. The road then runs north again (with a brief excursion inland to Bodmin Moor) and finishes with the cliffs and villages of North Devon. Though this is a route that can easily be followed by car or on foot, and will delight the lover of natural beauty, those who enjoy more strenuous exercise will find that too. During the last decade the Climbers' Club has shown great interest in the cliffs of Devon and Cornwall; they now have a splendid climbing hut, and publish the routes of ascent that can be tackled by members of the Club.

W.A. Poucher
4 Heathfield
Reigate Heath
Surrey
1984

Moor and valley

Dartmoor's brooding, heather-clad moors are cut with green and sheltered valleys, as seen here beneath a thundery sky. The gaunt old mineworkings date from the early nineteenth century and are a reminder of one of the last great industries of the county.

Two tors near Okehampton

Dartmoor, although a plateau, is scored by valleys both deep and shallow, and countless streams like this one run through them. The serenity of the scene is characteristic of the great moor.

View from Yes Tor
(overleaf)

Yes Tor is one of the highest points on Dartmoor (2,028 ft) – a granite outcrop that yields this breathtaking view. It lies within the Ministry of Defence Firing Range, but is sometimes accessible to the public. Just below the tor can be seen Meldon Viaduct and the limestone quarries.

Vixen Tor

The road from Tavistock to Two Bridges, the B3357, passes this striking natural monument – the highest rock mass on Dartmoor.

Vixen Tor from the south

Because the ground level is 40 ft lower than on the north (see previous picture) the rocks here tower an awe-inspiring 90 ft above the visitor.

Standing stones at Merrivale

(overleaf)

Merrivale, in the parish of Walkhampton, abounds in prehistoric remains: cairns, kistvaens, a stone circle, and menhirs. But the purpose behind this row of stones remains a mystery. They are to your right on the B3357, not far from Vixen Tor.

Two Bridges

This beautiful little spot in the centre of Dartmoor National Park takes its name from the presence of two bridges over the West Dart – the one seen in this picture, and a clapper bridge that was moved in 1772 to cross the West Dart below its junction with the Cowsic.

Dartmeet

(overleaf)

Continuing along the B3357 from Tavistock, you will come to Dartmeet which also has two bridges. This peaceful rural scene shows the more recent bridge.

The old clapper bridge at Dartmeet

This primitive type of bridge, composed of huge stones, superseded the even older method of stream-crossing: stepping stones. The clapper bridge at Dartmeet is one of the four largest in Devon.

Rippon Tor

This imposing mass of rocks to the south-east of
Widecombe-in-the-Moor rises to a height of
1,563 ft above sea-level.

Haytor and Saddle Tor
(overleaf)

These two majestic tors, seen here from Hemsworth Gate, stand sentinel over the lonely moorland.

The west face of Haytor
(overleaf pp 34/35)

Haytor is the most popular and best known tor on Dartmoor because of its spectacular position. One one side of it the land falls away dramatically, and from here the visitor can familiarize himself with the Dartmoor landscape.

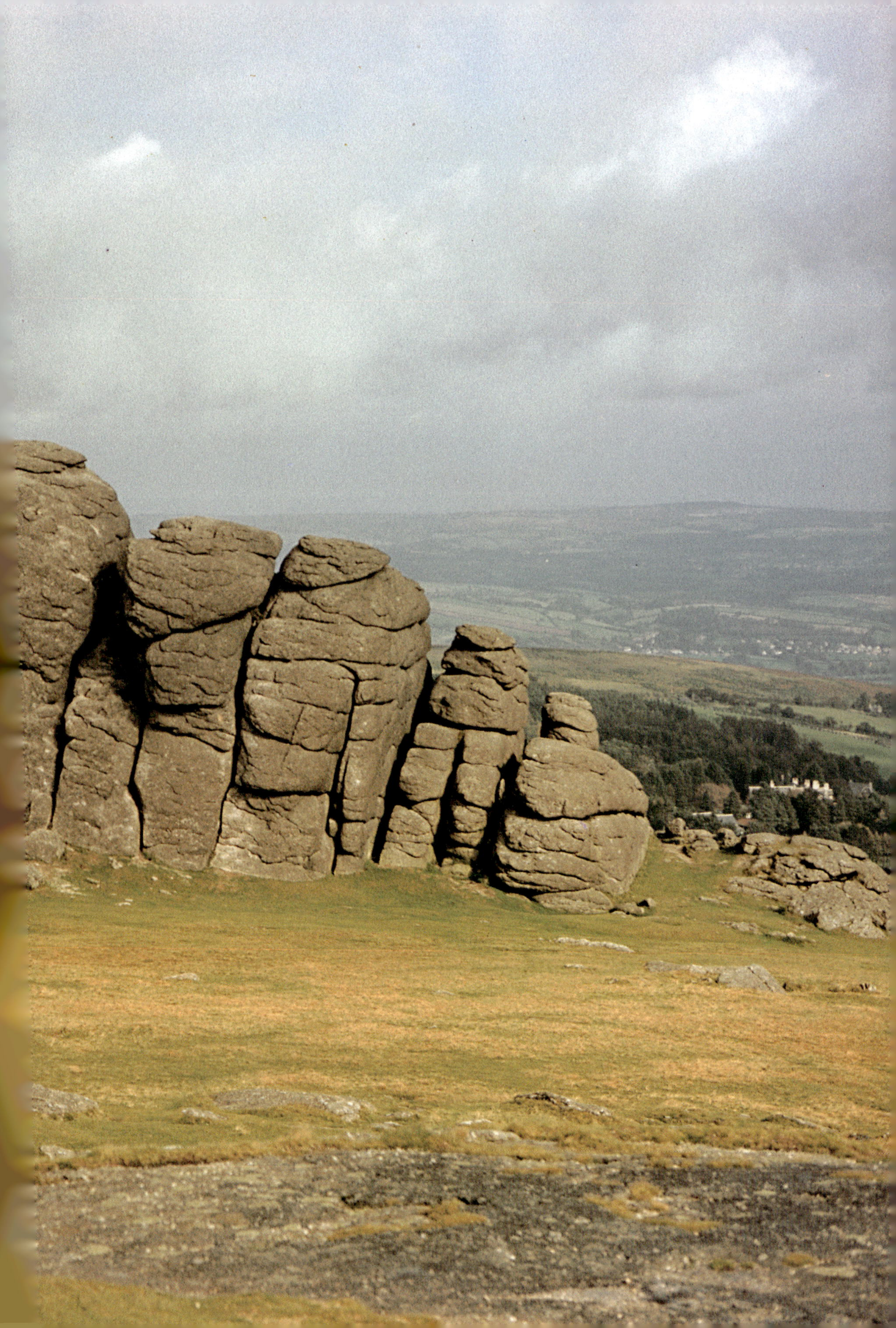

Climbing Haytor

Care should be taken when climbing this massive pile of curving rocks: they can be very slippery.

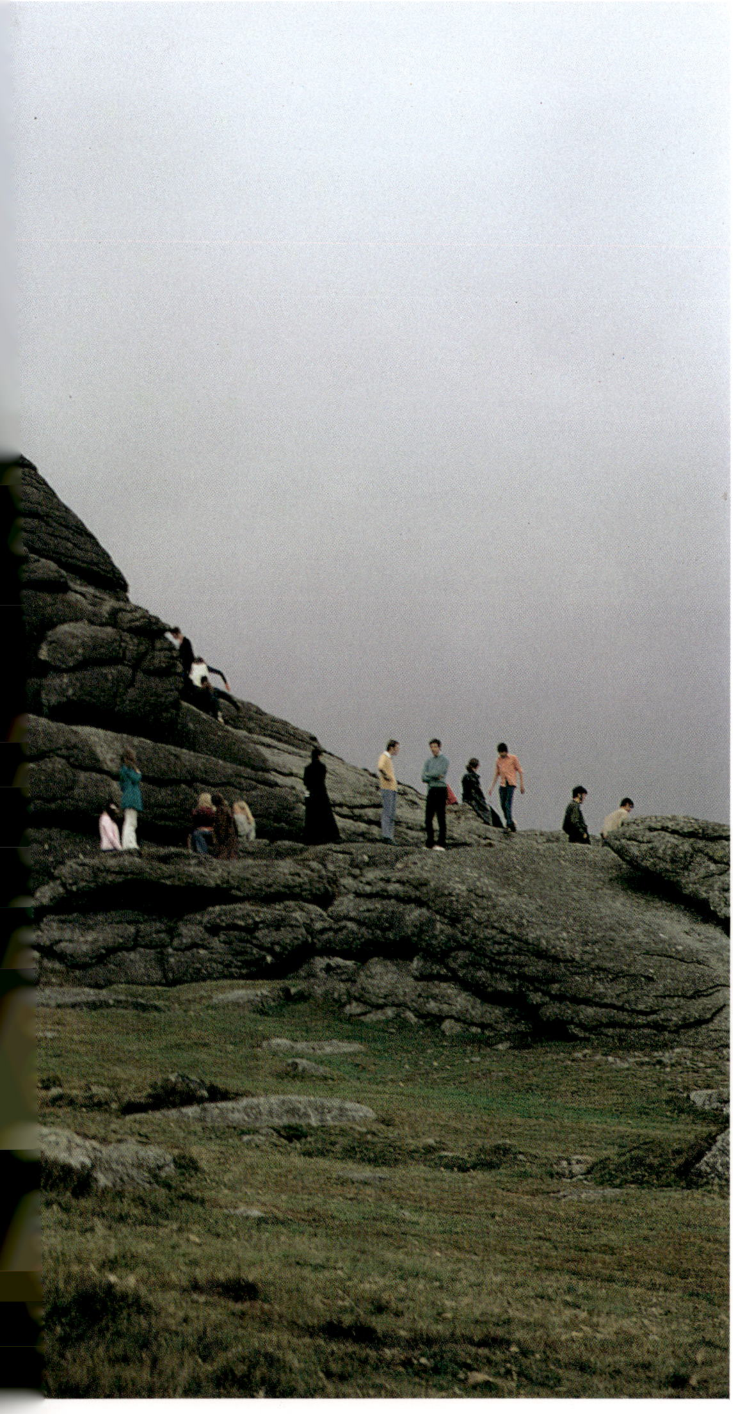

Haytor Rocks

Blue granite is quarried near Haytor, and a few hundred yards north-east of the rocks is a massive quarry from which runs a double line of grooved stone blocks – the Haytor 'granite railway', dating from the nineteenth century.

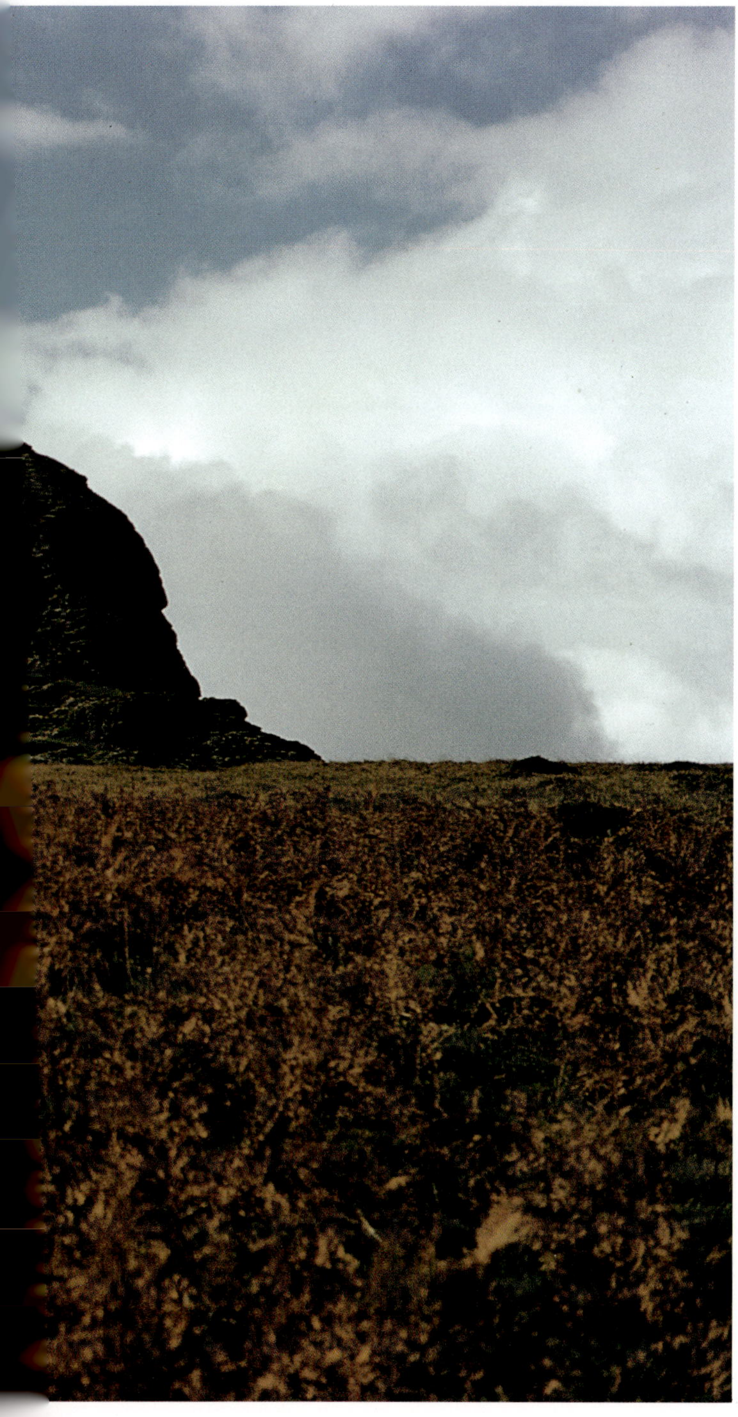

Bonehill Rocks
(here and overleaf)

Two views of this jumble of immense rocks rising from the bracken, which is an outcrop of coarse granite to the north-west of Haytor.

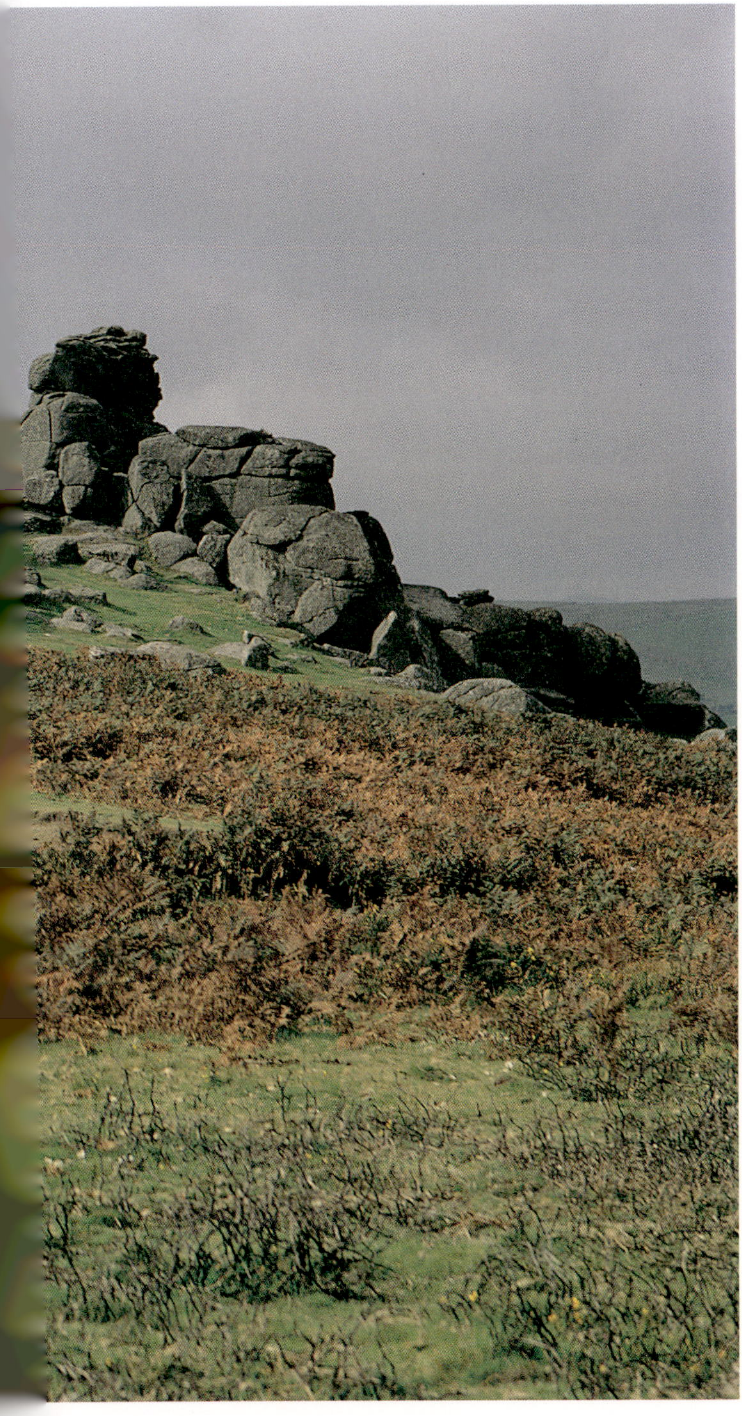

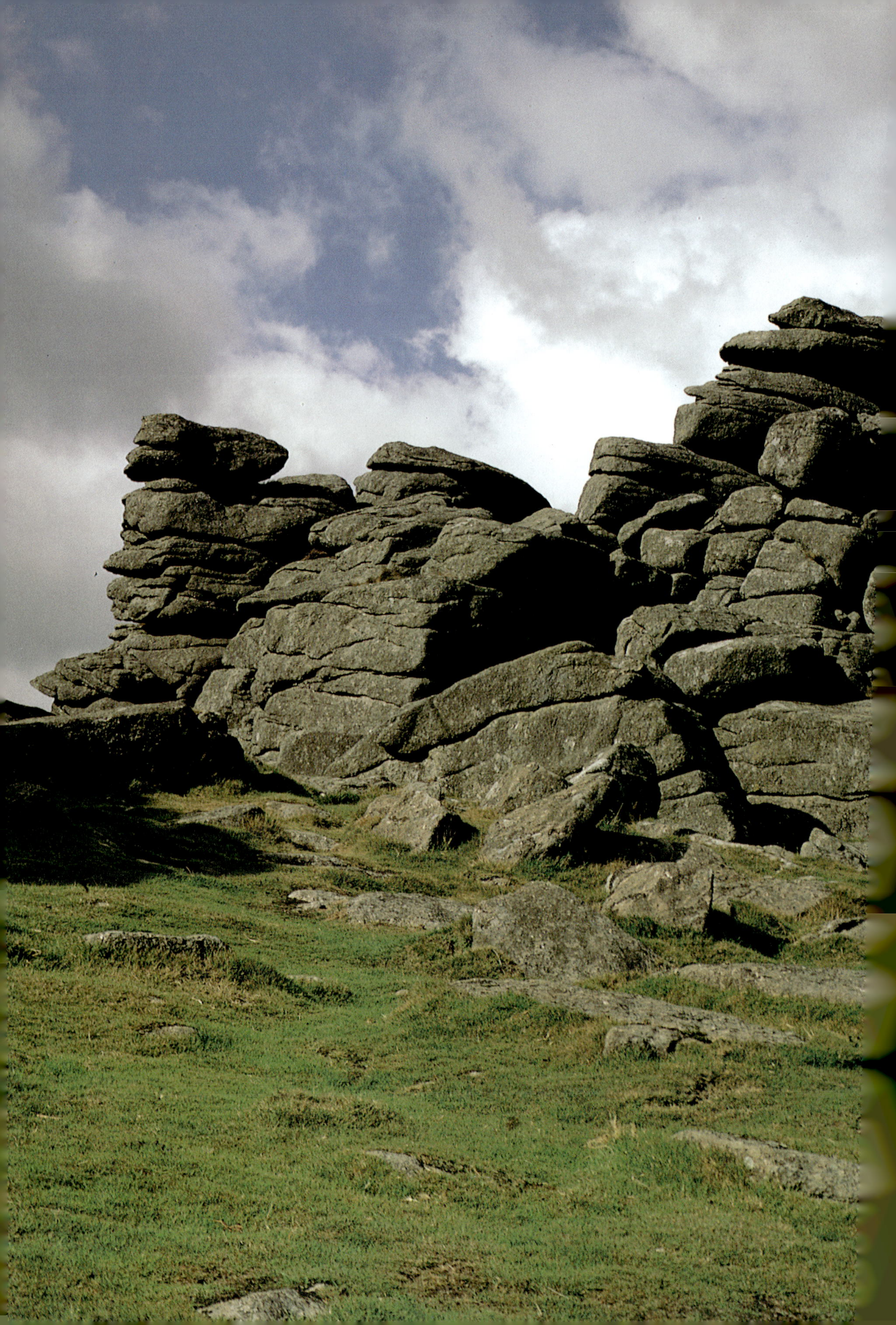

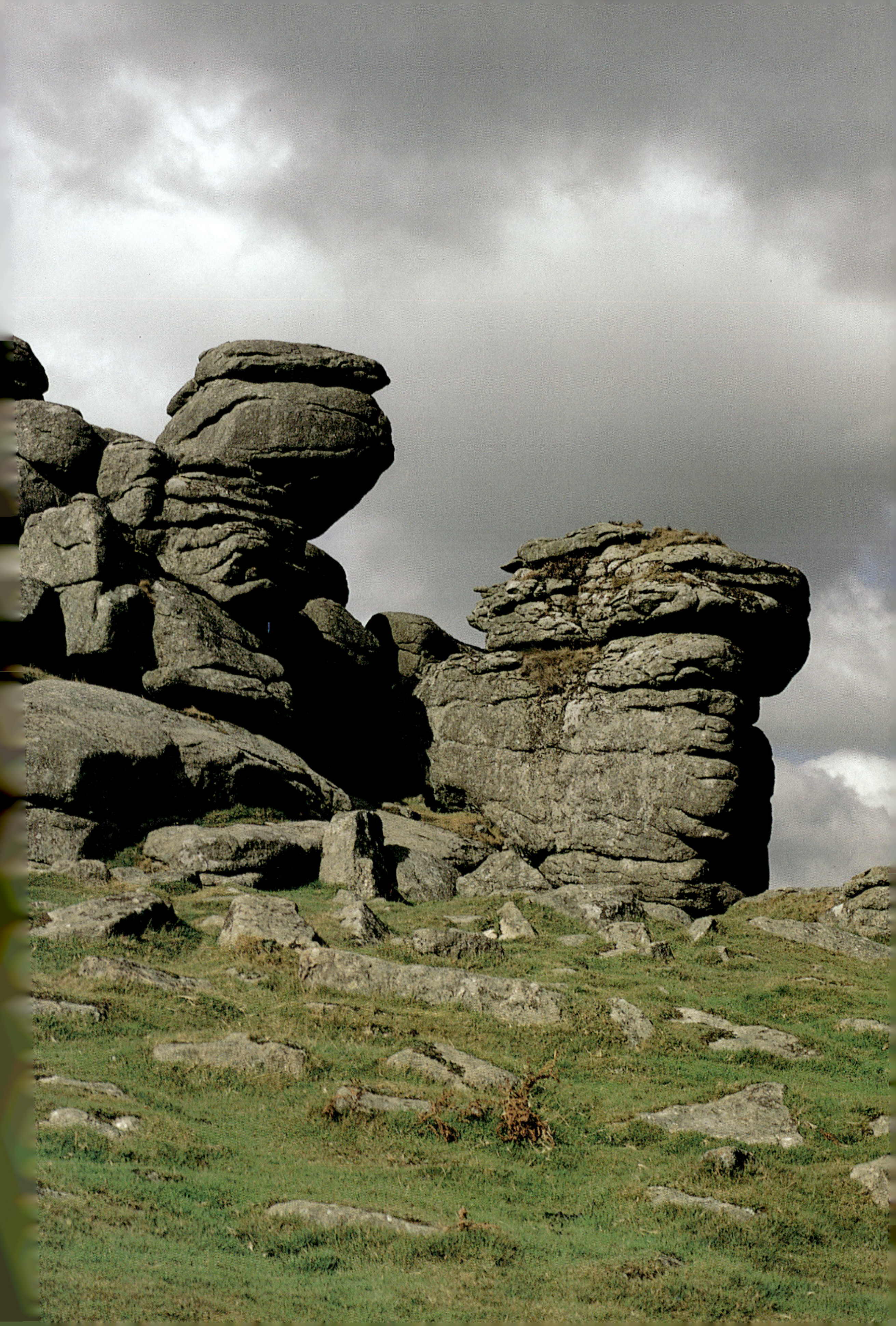

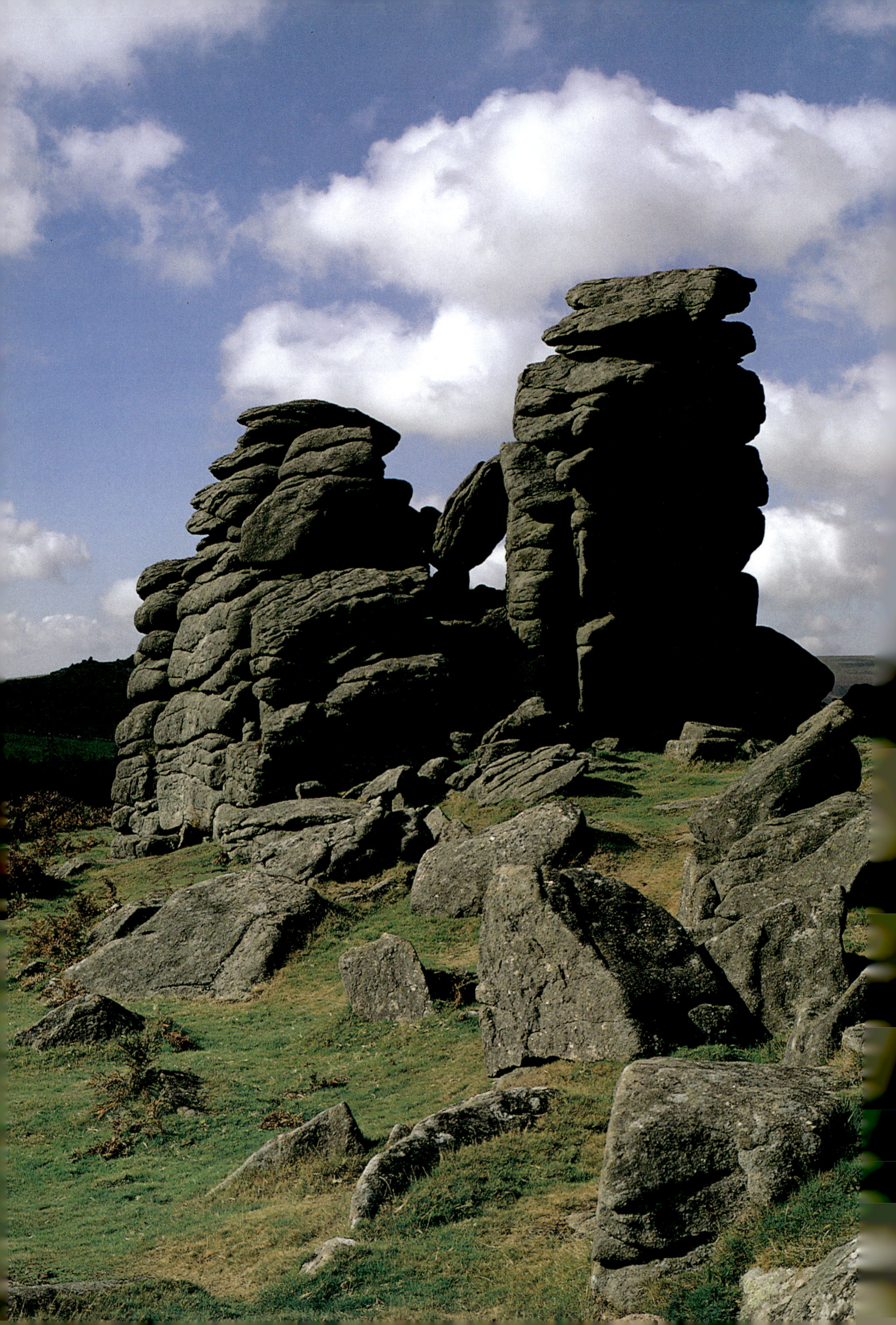

Hound Tor

This, in my opinion, is the tor most likely to interest the photographer, because of its lofty elevation, fine rock architecture, and splendid isolation.

Hound Tor in autumn

(overleaf)

The rich tapestry of autumn colours makes a splendid background to these rocks on a fine October day.

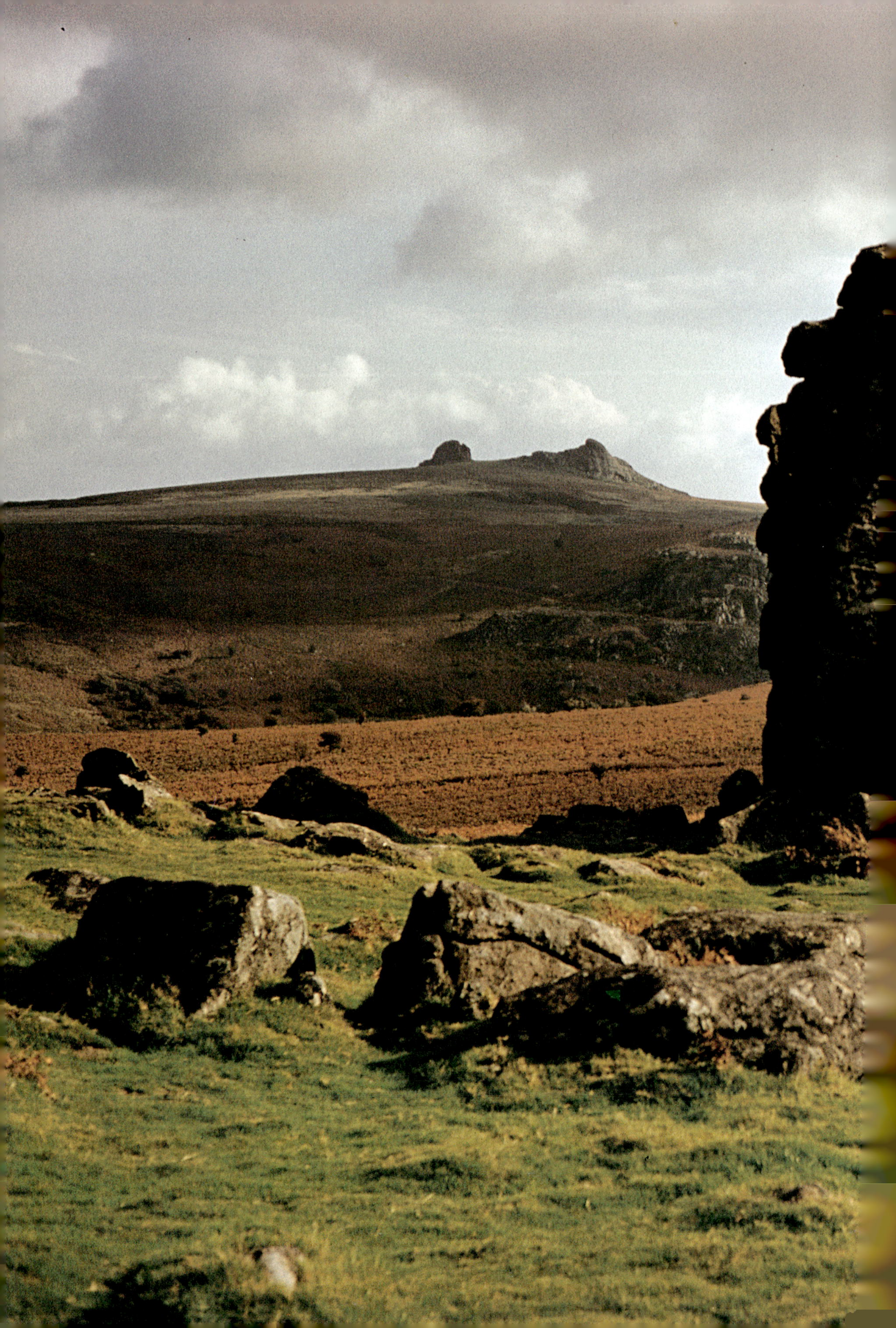

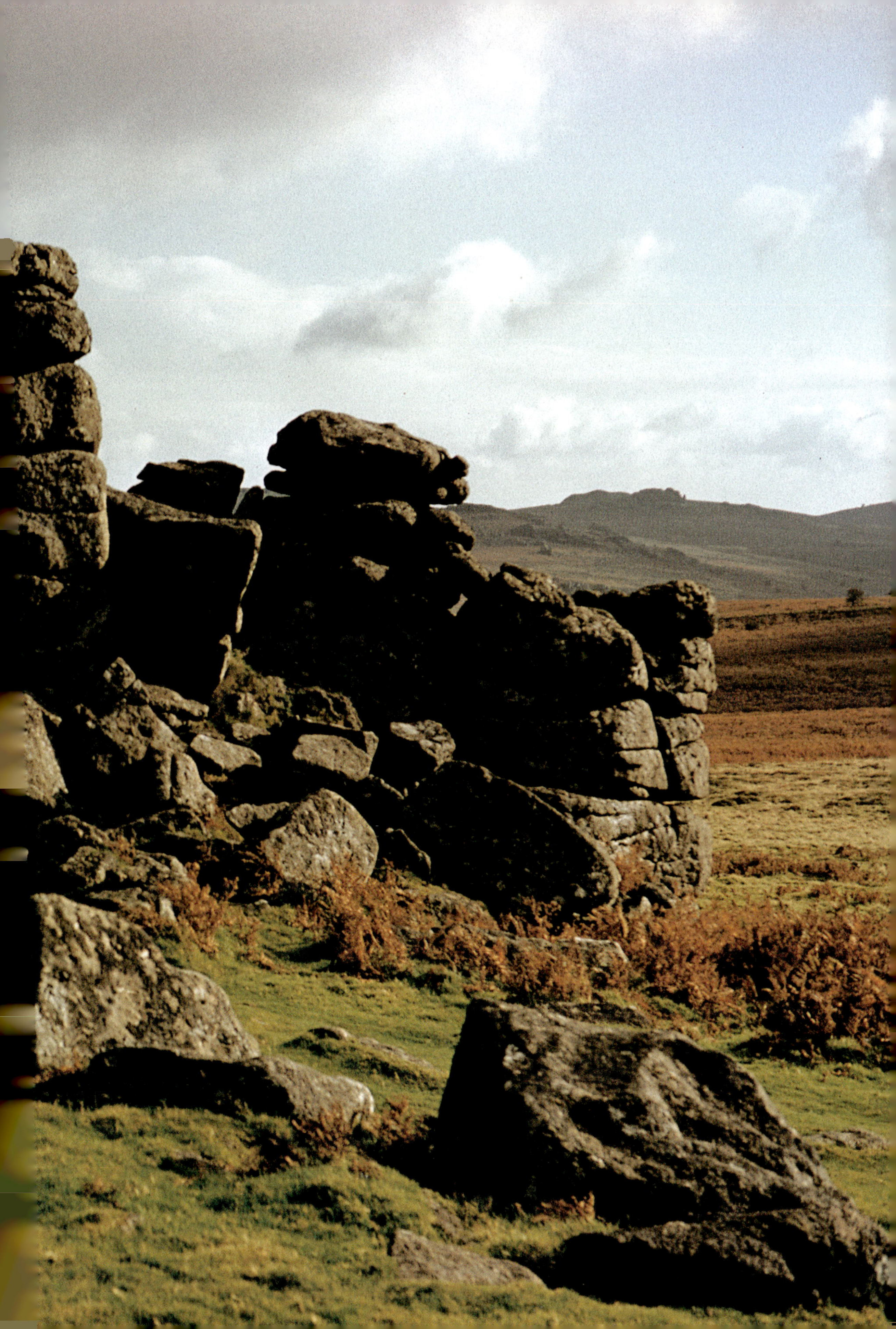

Hound Tor's prehistoric past

Traces of ancient Britain have been found near this tor, including a kistvaen (or lidded stone slab grave) and a retaining circle of stones.

Bowerman's Nose
(overleaf)

This grotesque column of granite near Manaton, rising in places to 26 ft high, has been eroded in such a way as to delight all who discover it.

Grimspound
(overleaf pp 52/53)

This Bronze Age hut circle, lying about 2½ miles from Widecombe-in-the-Moor, covers almost four acres, and has twenty-four hut circles enclosed within it.

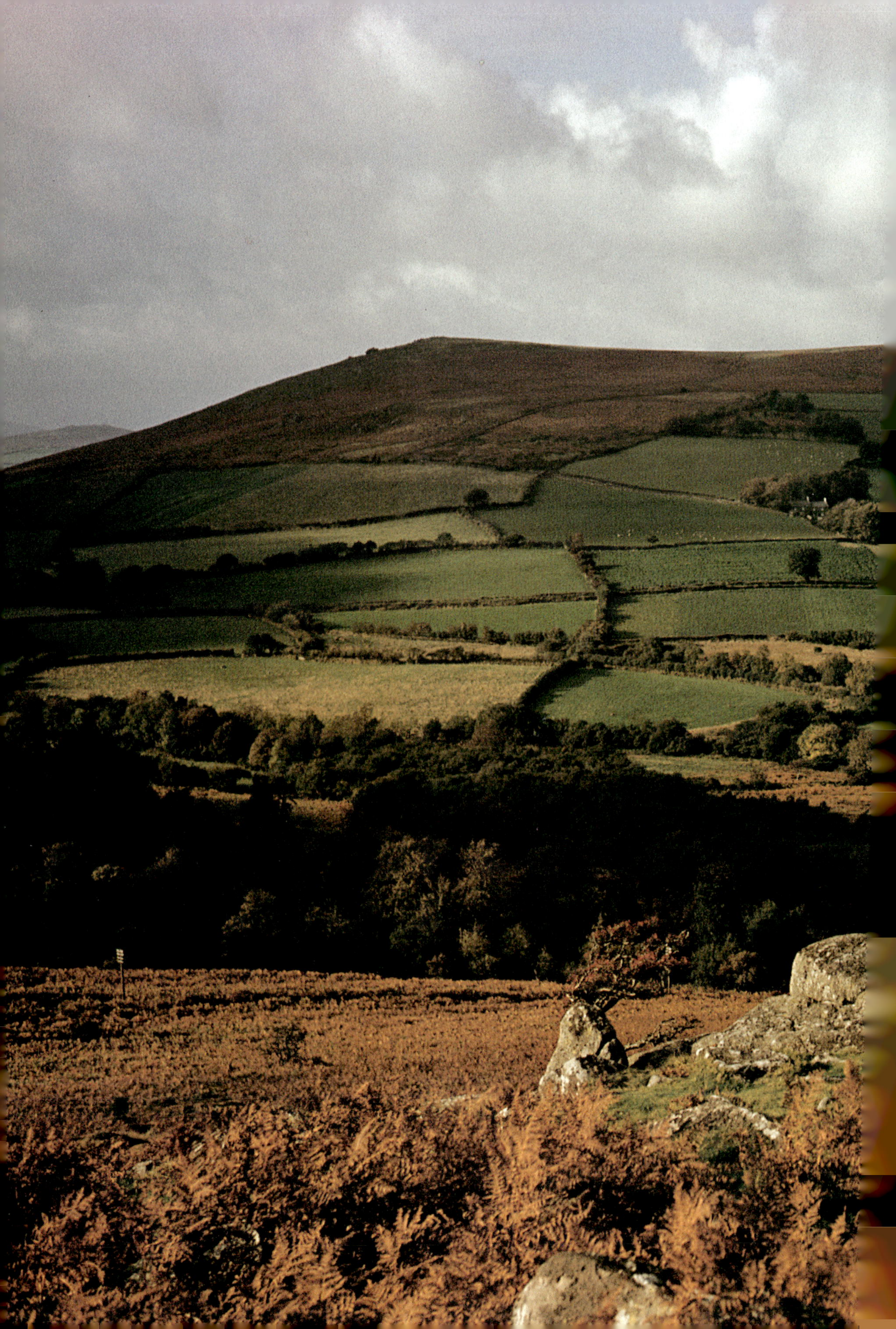

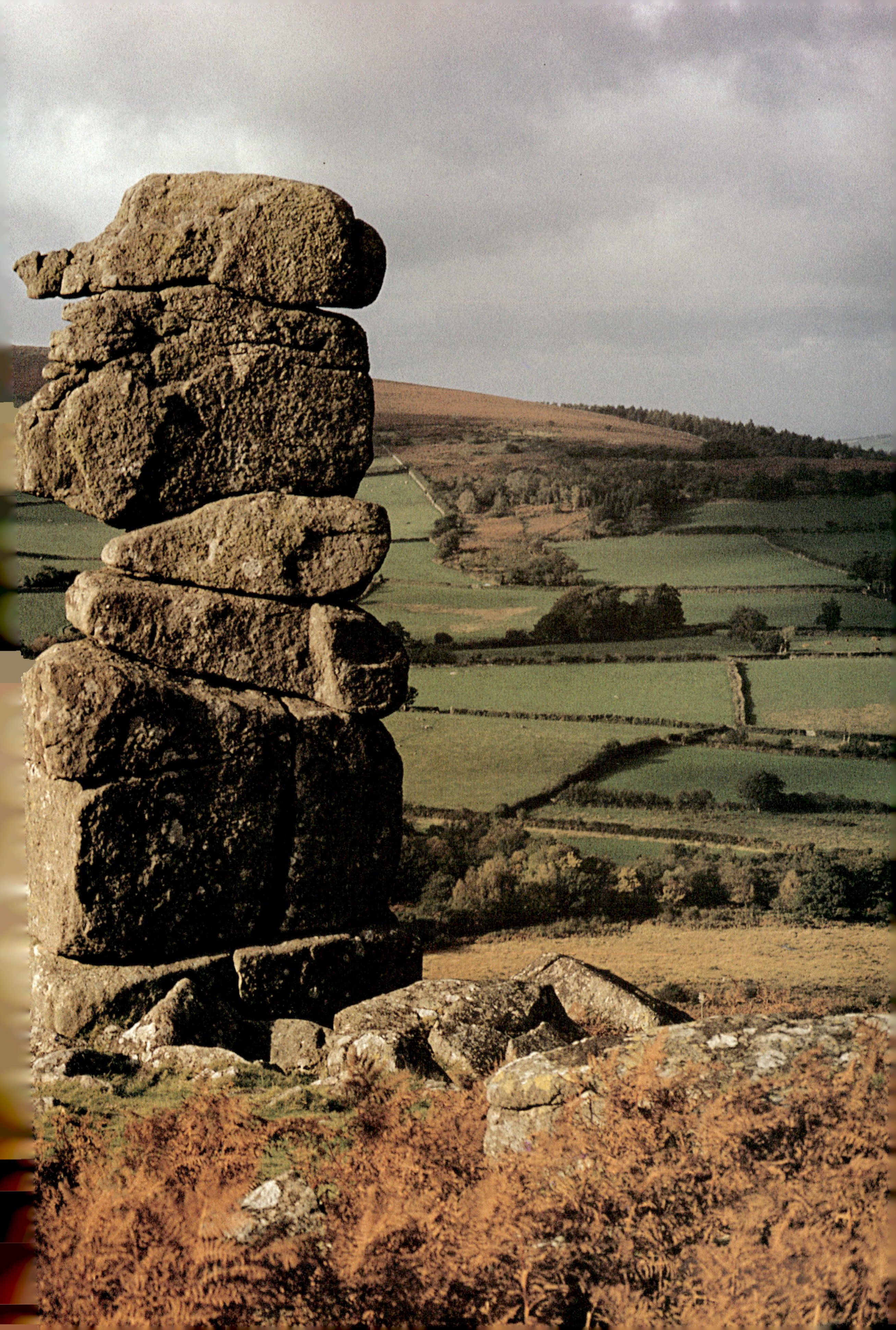

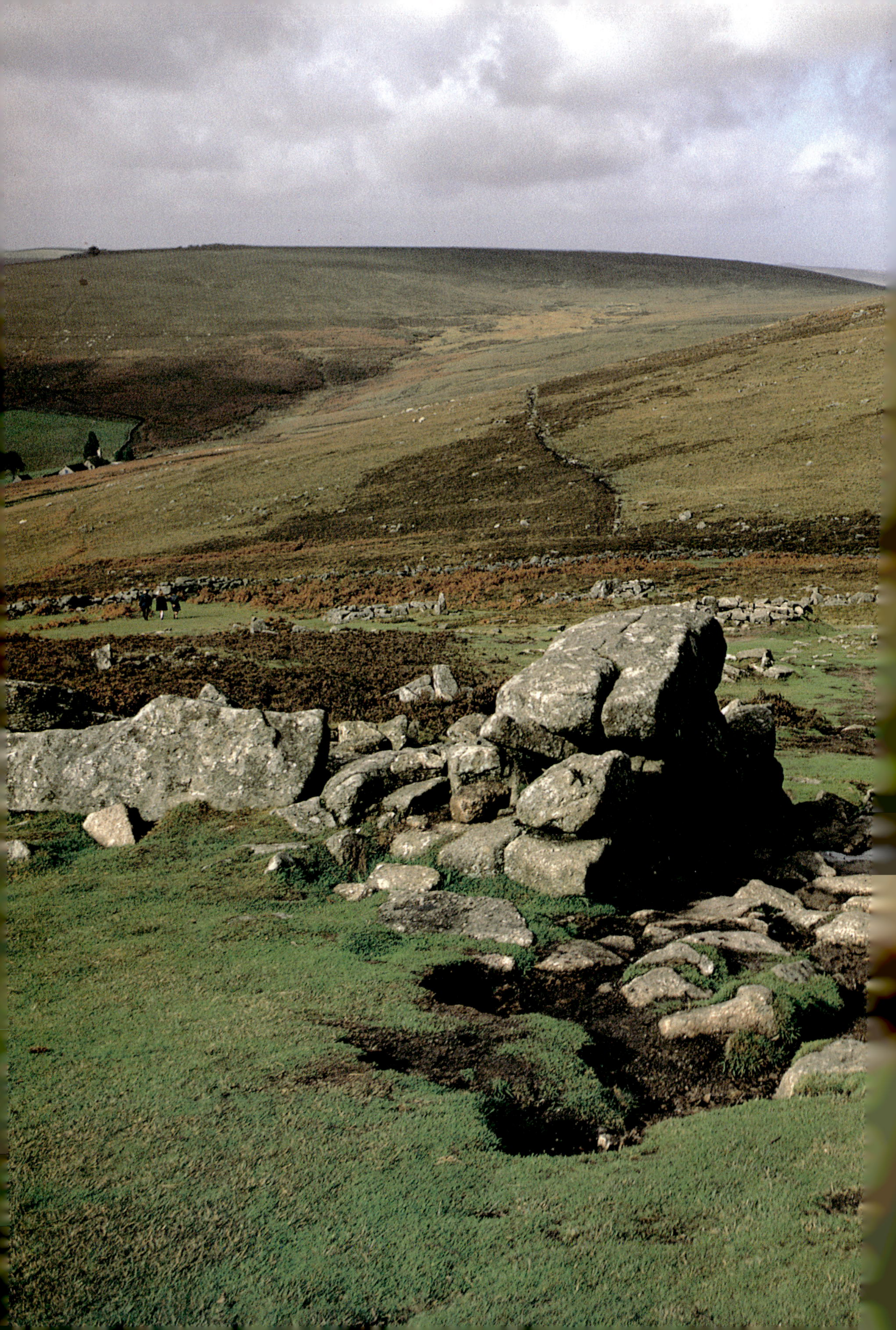

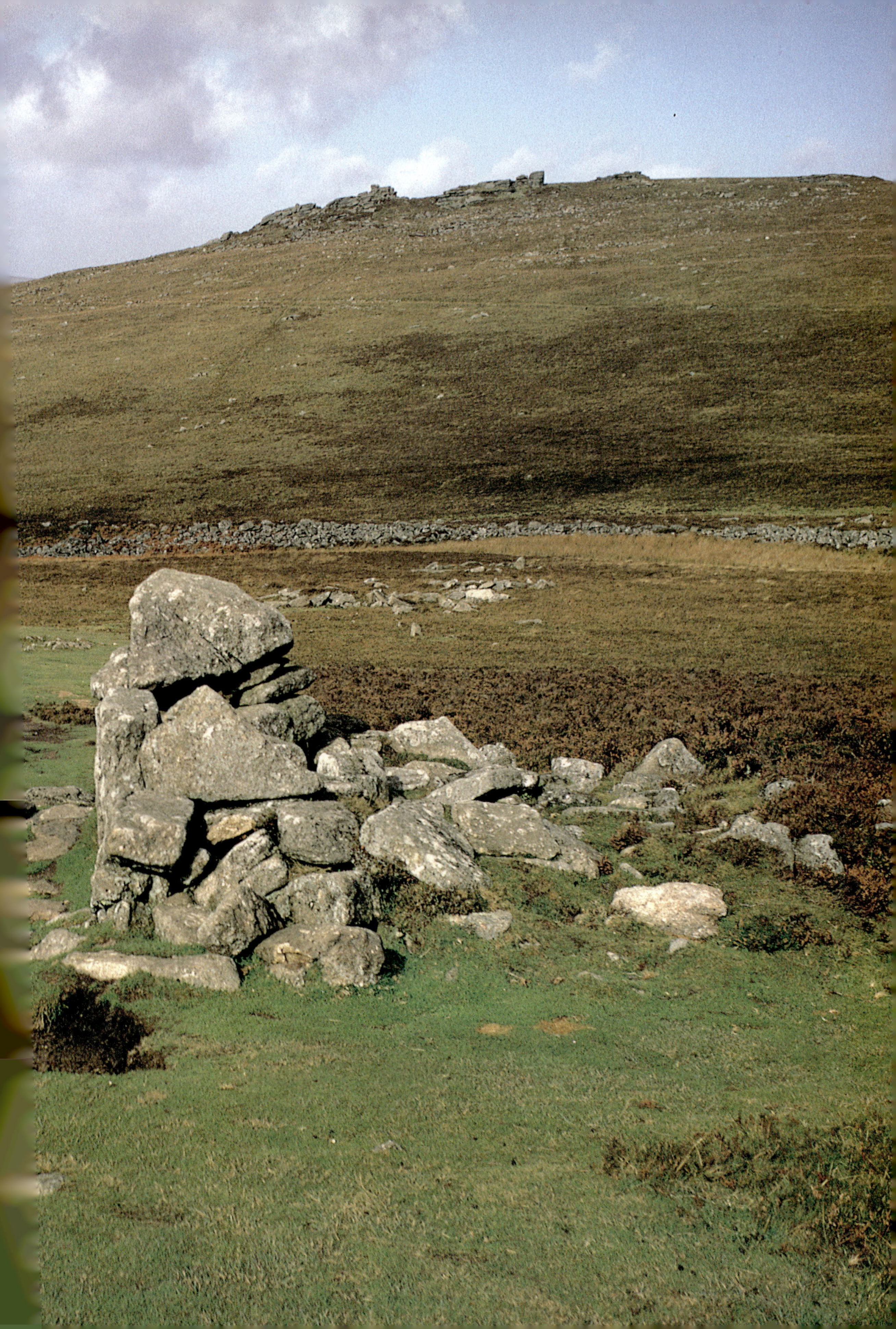

Bennett's Cross, near Grimspound

This old granite cross in the midst of Dartmoor once marked a medieval track across the moorland wastes, before the road was built.

Postbridge
(overleaf)

This is one of the most famous beauty spots on Dartmoor, with the old clapper bridge spanning a quiet river lined by lovely beeches.

Wild ponies
(overleaf pp 58/59)

Bracken, which covers vast tracts of Dartmoor where the friendly ponies wander, turns the landscape to gold in autumn.

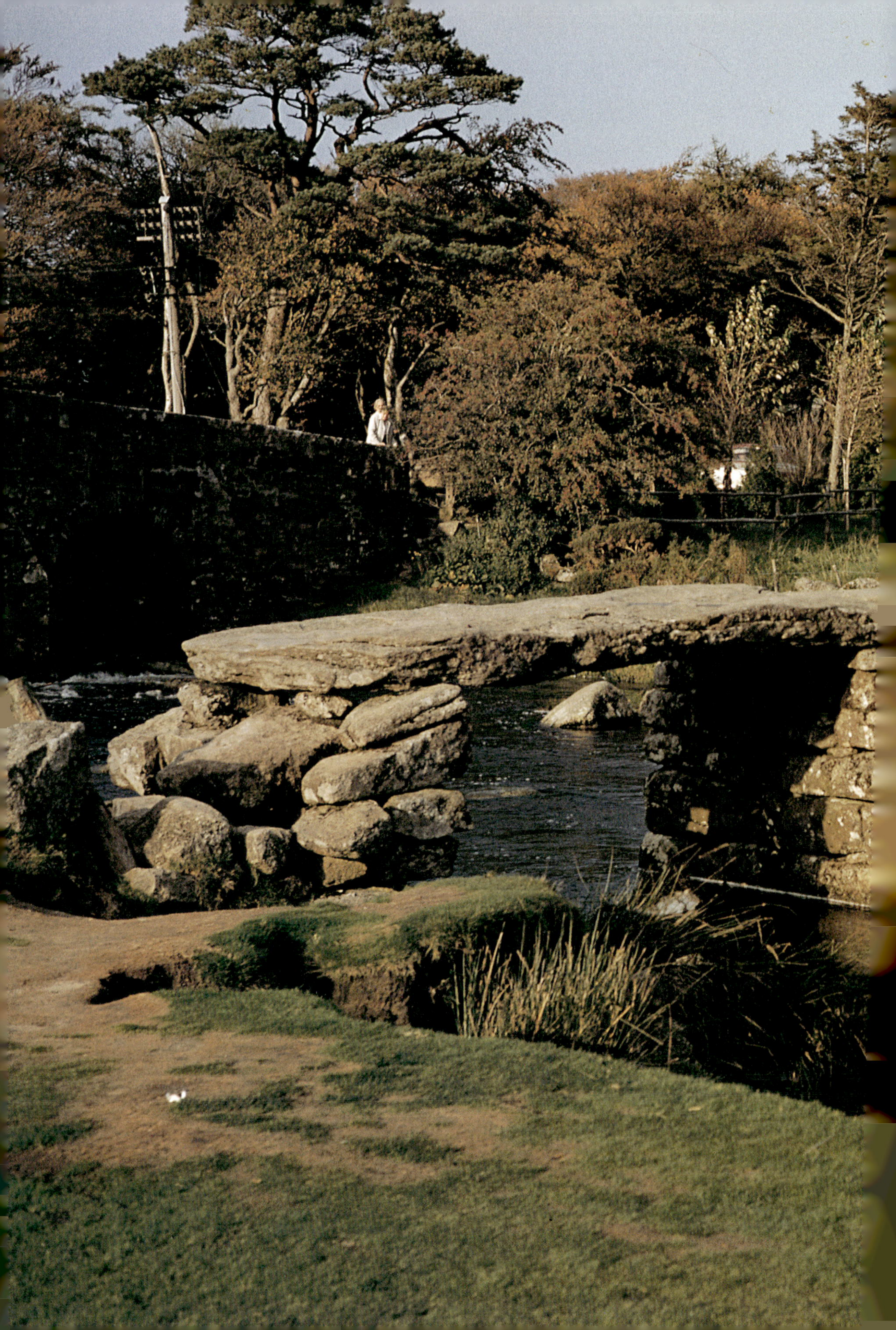

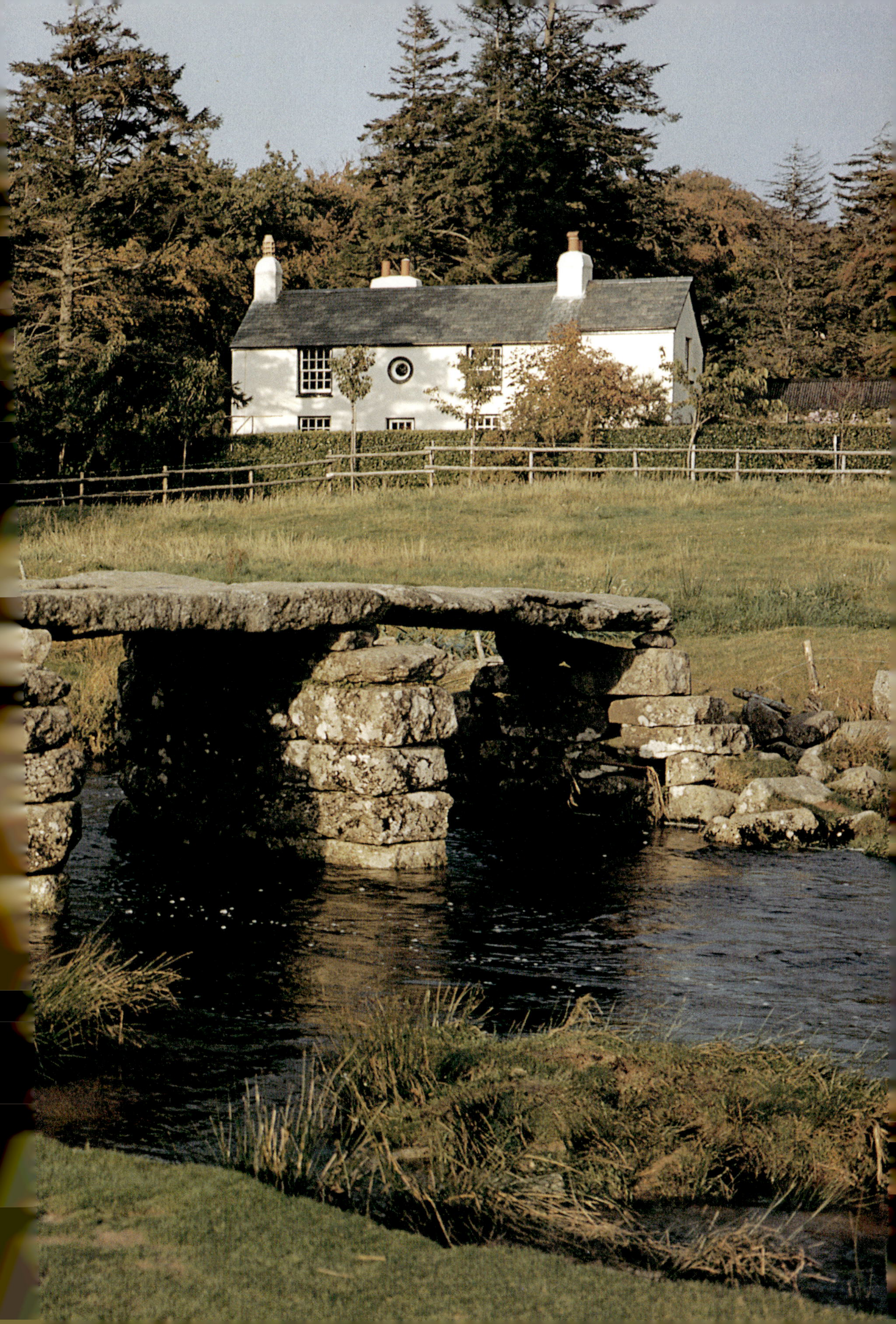

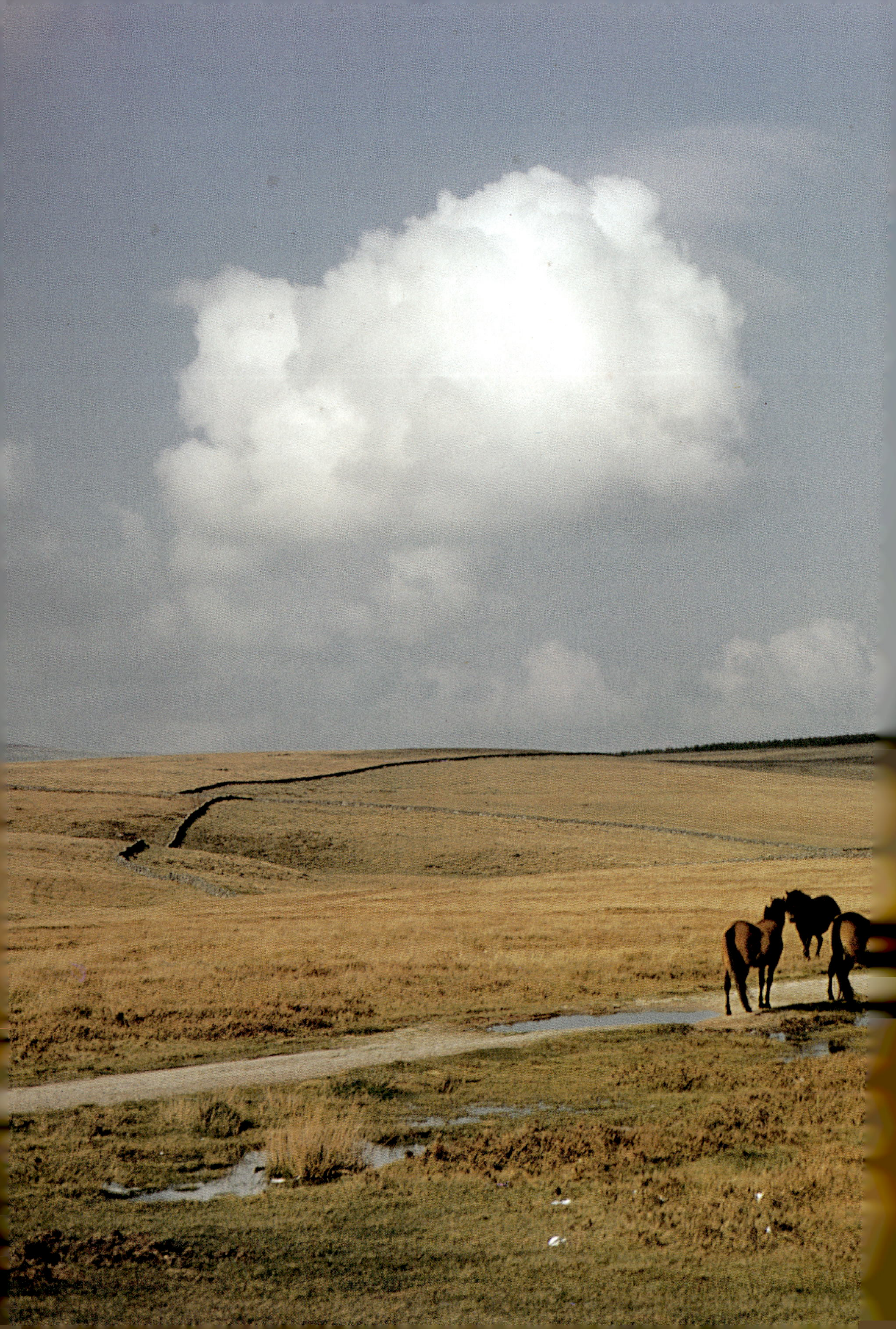

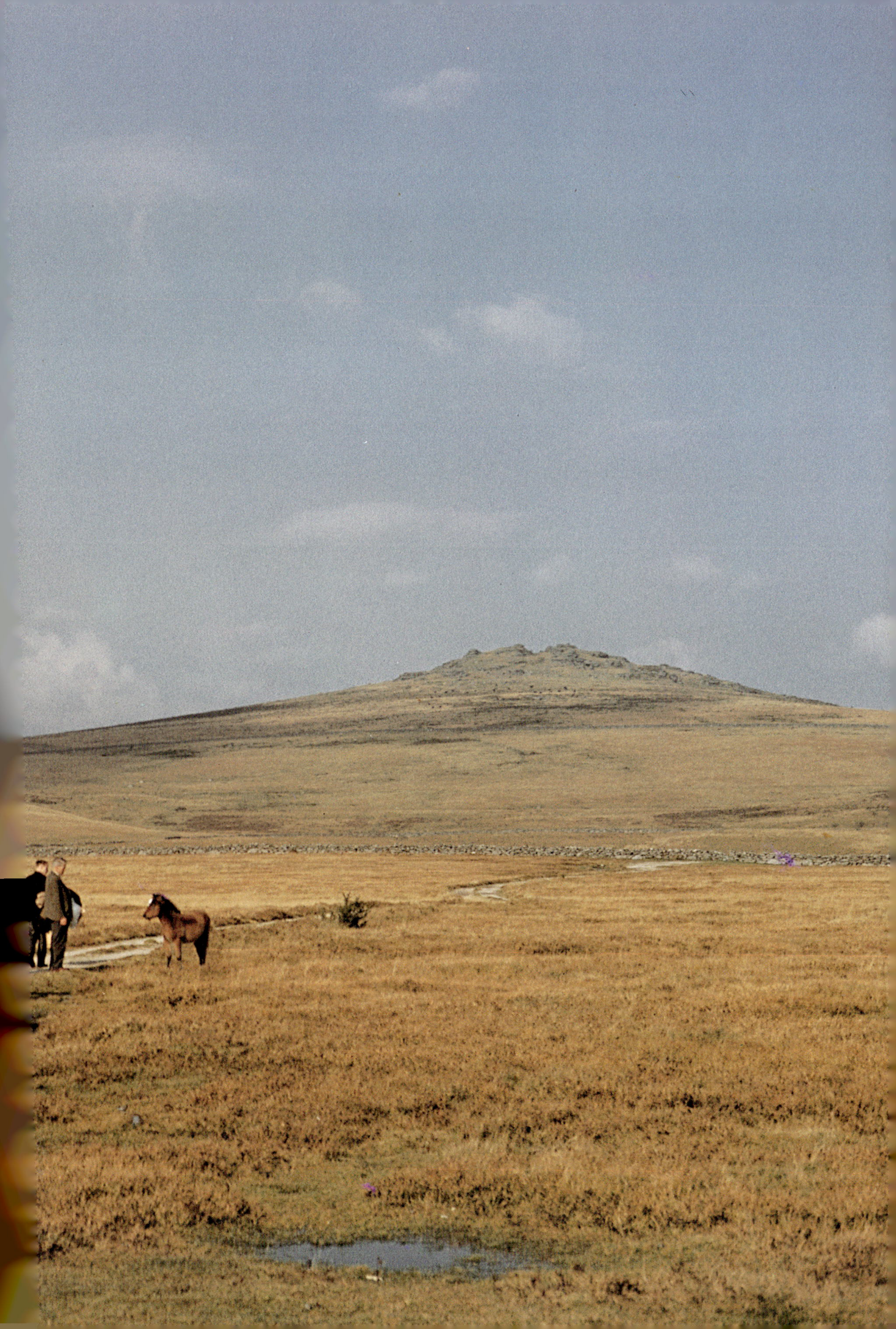

The Devon coast

The cliffs towering over the shingle beach near Sidmouth glow pink in the light of the evening sun.

The Cornish coast
(overleaf and pp 64/65)

Compare the red cliffs and narrow shingle beach seen left with the magnificent beach of firm, clean sand, nearly 3 miles long, at Perranporth on the north Cornish coast. Facing the Atlantic rollers, Perranporth is noted for its surf bathing, and for the archways, caves and pools formed by rocks and tides.

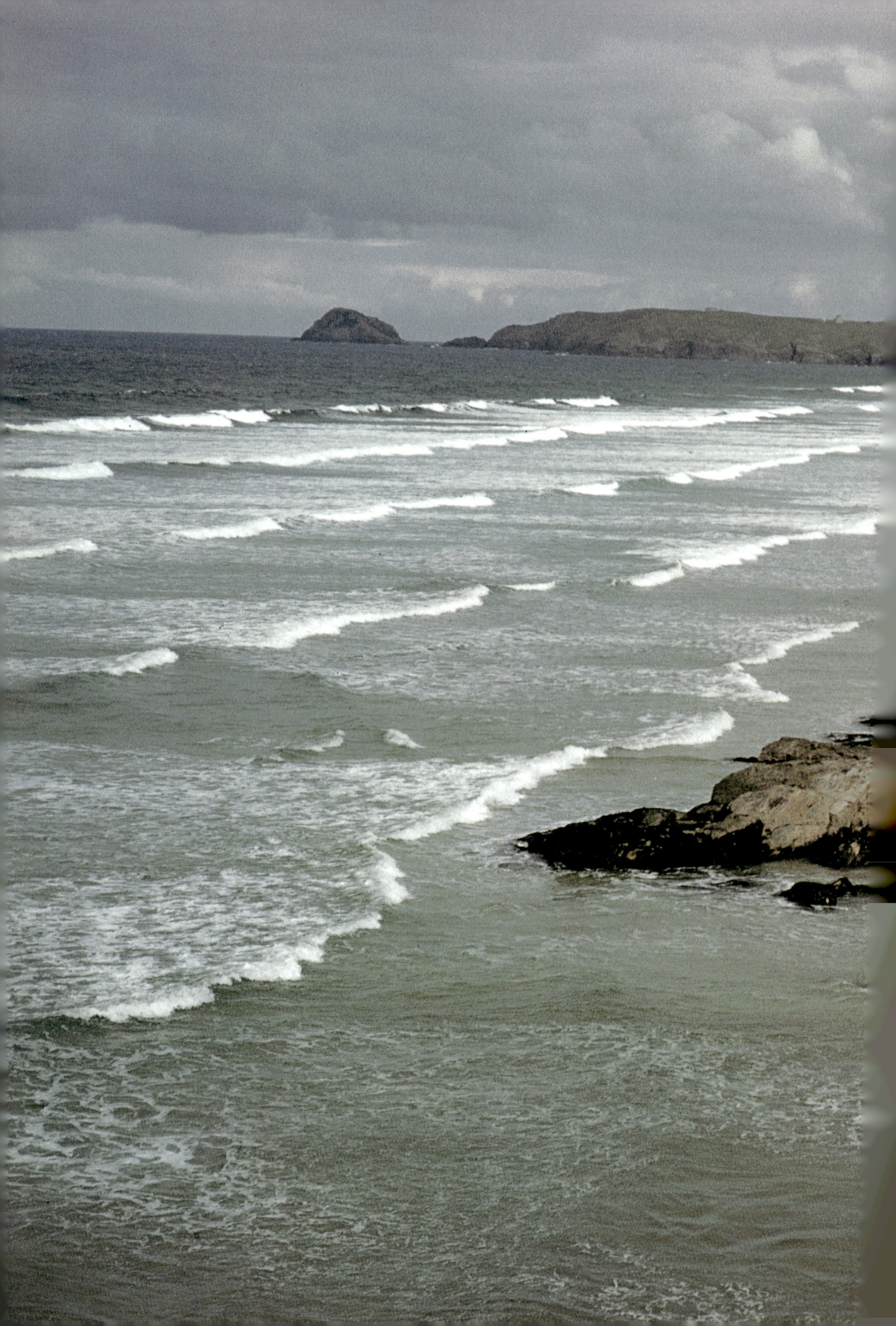

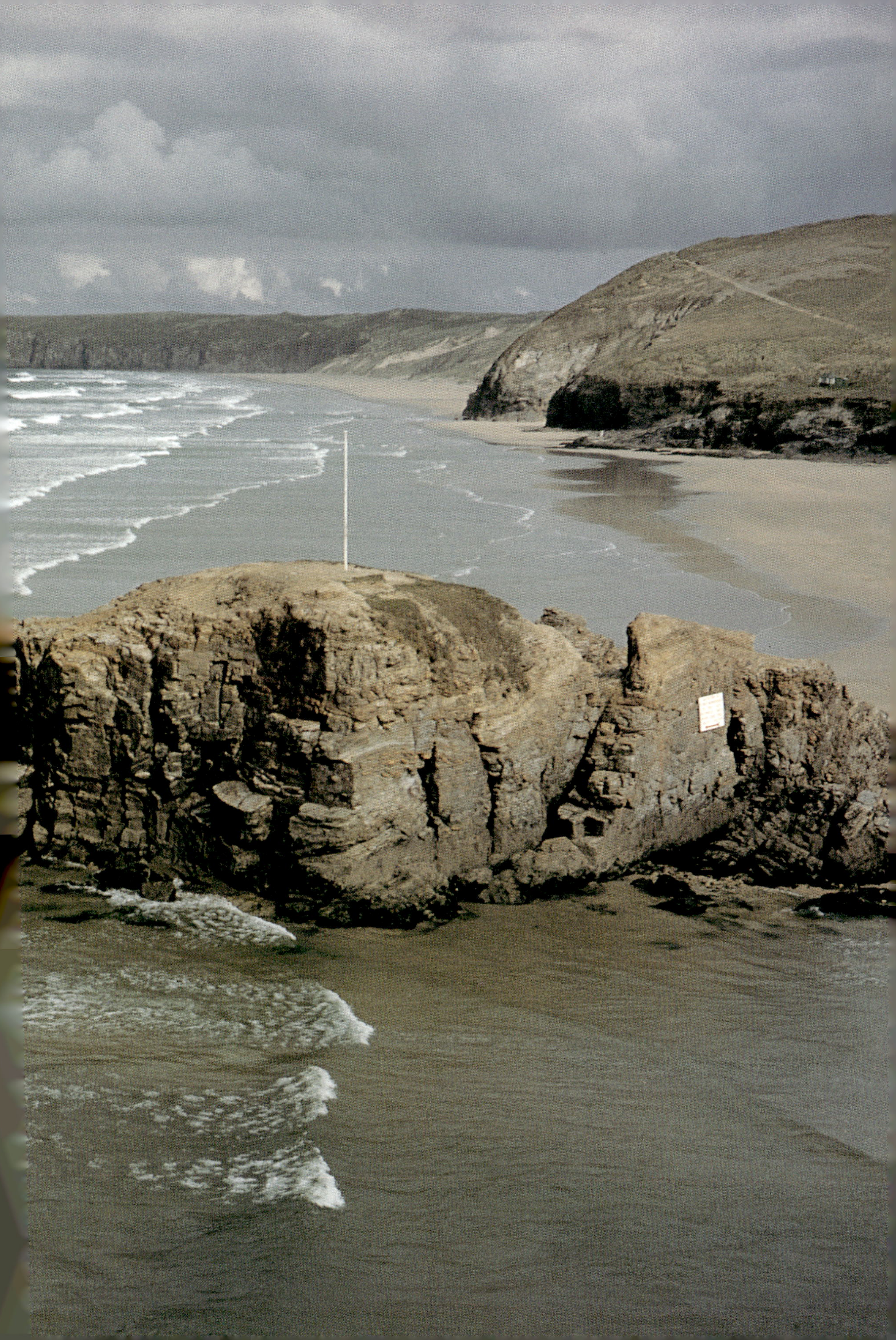

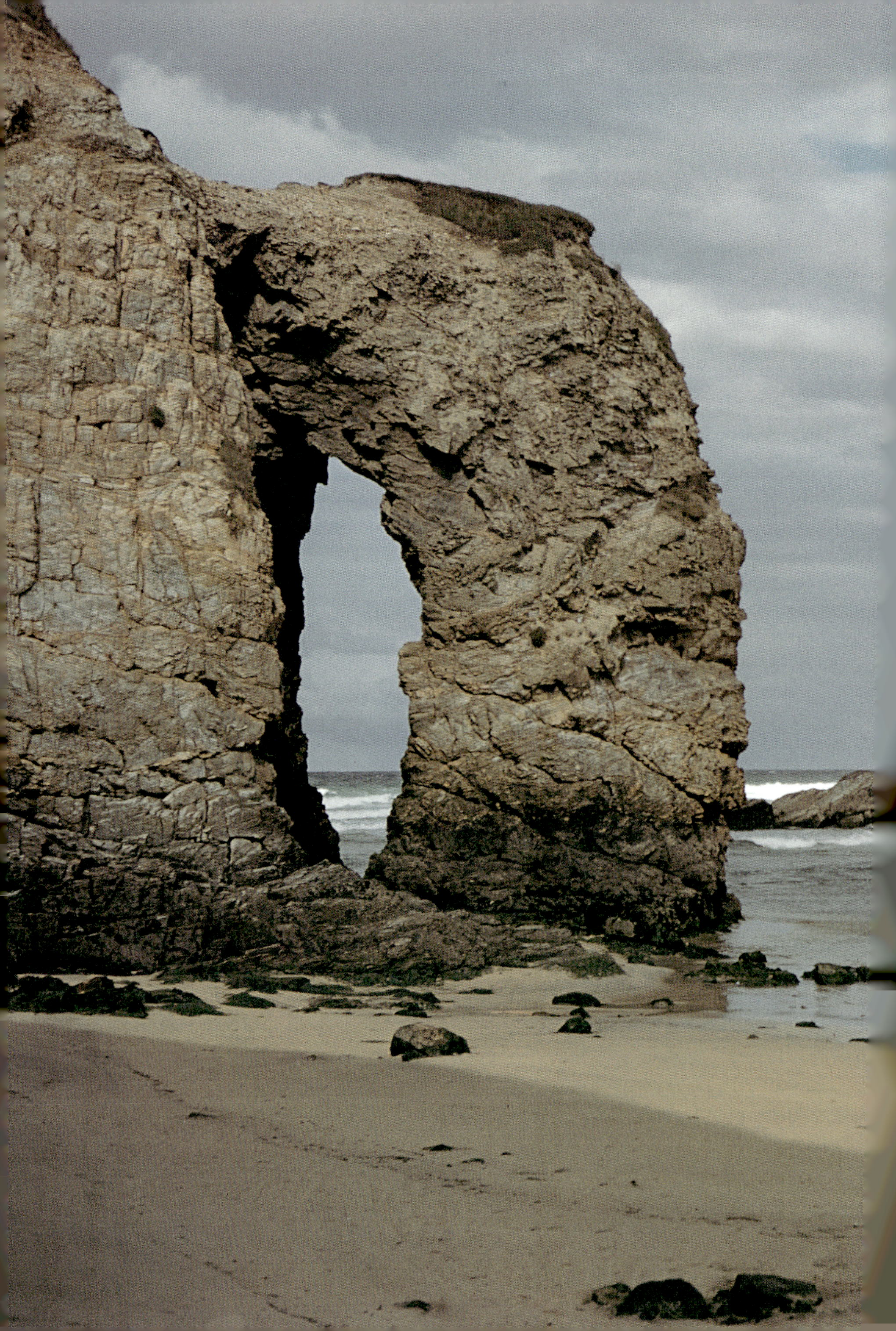

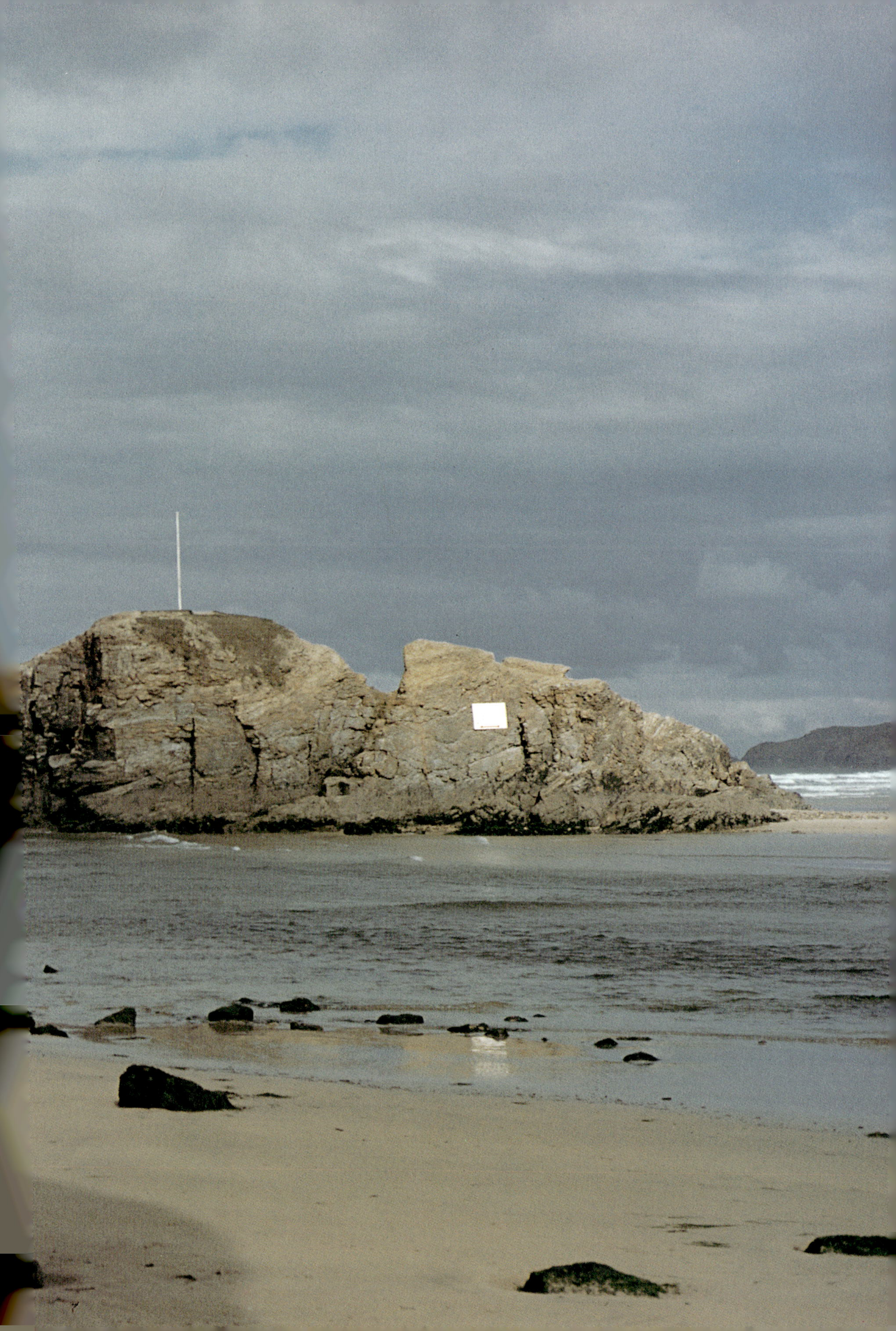

Teignmouth

The estuary of the River Teign, on which this resort is built, offers splendid sport to the sailor, the windsurfer, or the fisherman.

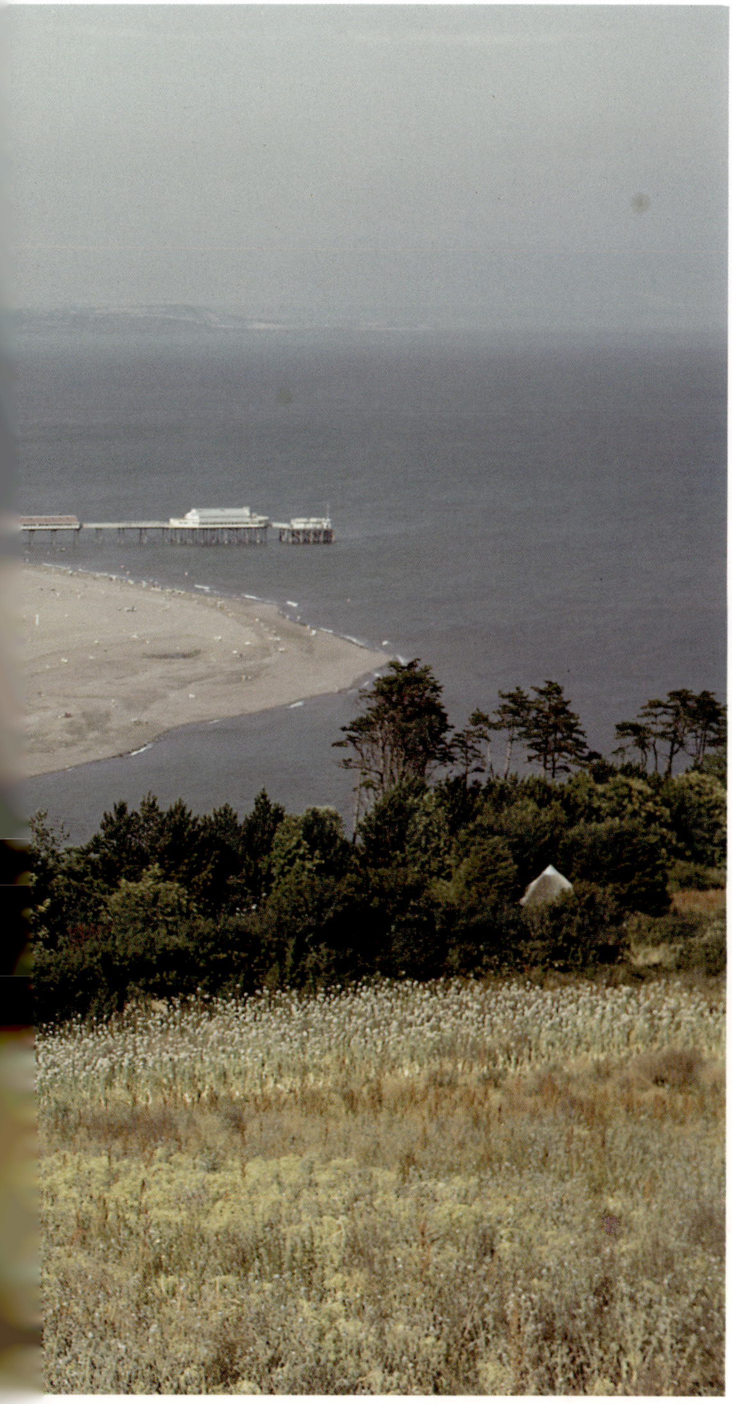

Shaldon

Across the estuary from busy Teignmouth, this beautiful little place has a timeless, unspoilt charm.

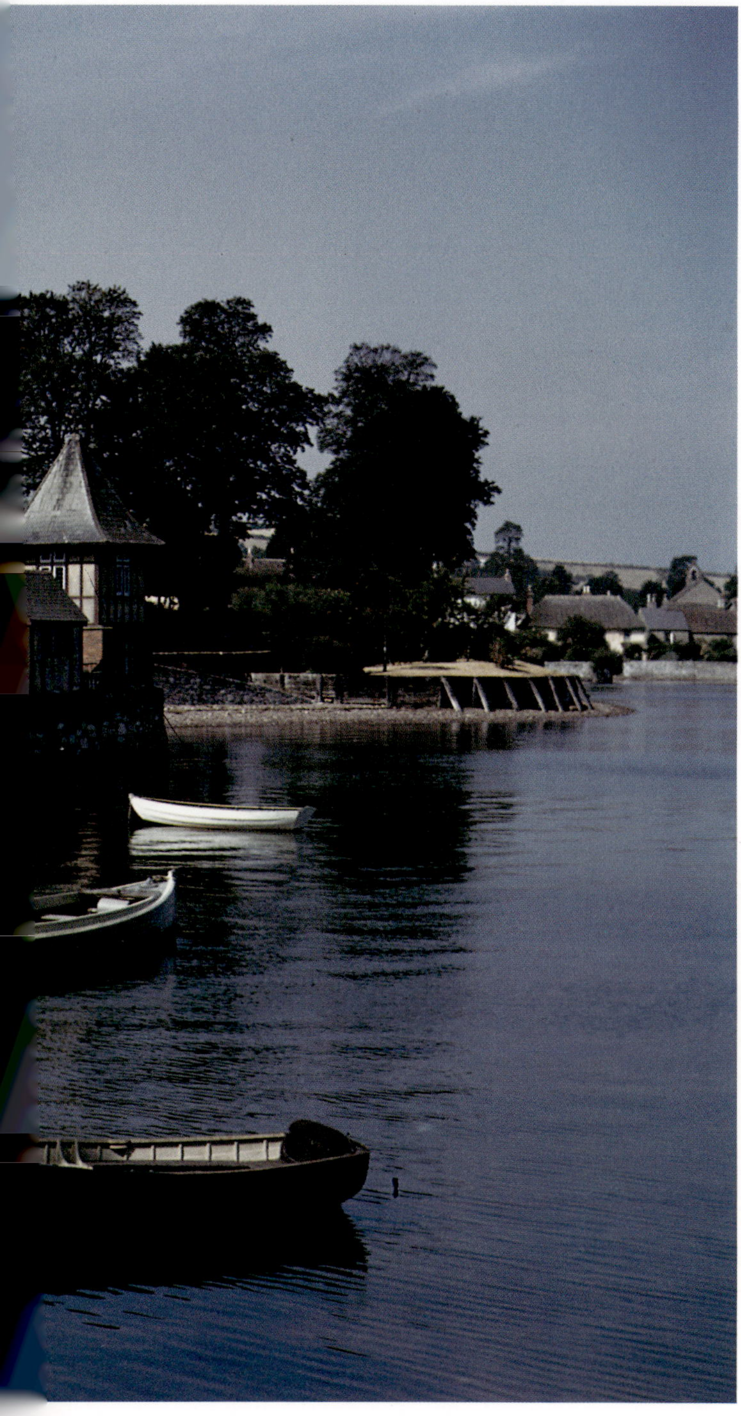

Hope Cove

Lying between Salcombe and Thurlestone, this little resort is sheltered by the bulk of Bolt Tail to the south-west.

Thurlestone

(overleaf)

Here steep cliffs give way to low ones, and sandy beaches afford pleasant picnicking for holidaymakers. The well-known arched rock, after which Thurlestone ('holed stone') is named, can be seen in the bay.

East Looe

(overleaf pp 74/75)

The quayside of this small Cornish fishing port is seen here across the river from the village of West Looe. East Looe is now famous as a centre for deepsea- and shark-fishing.

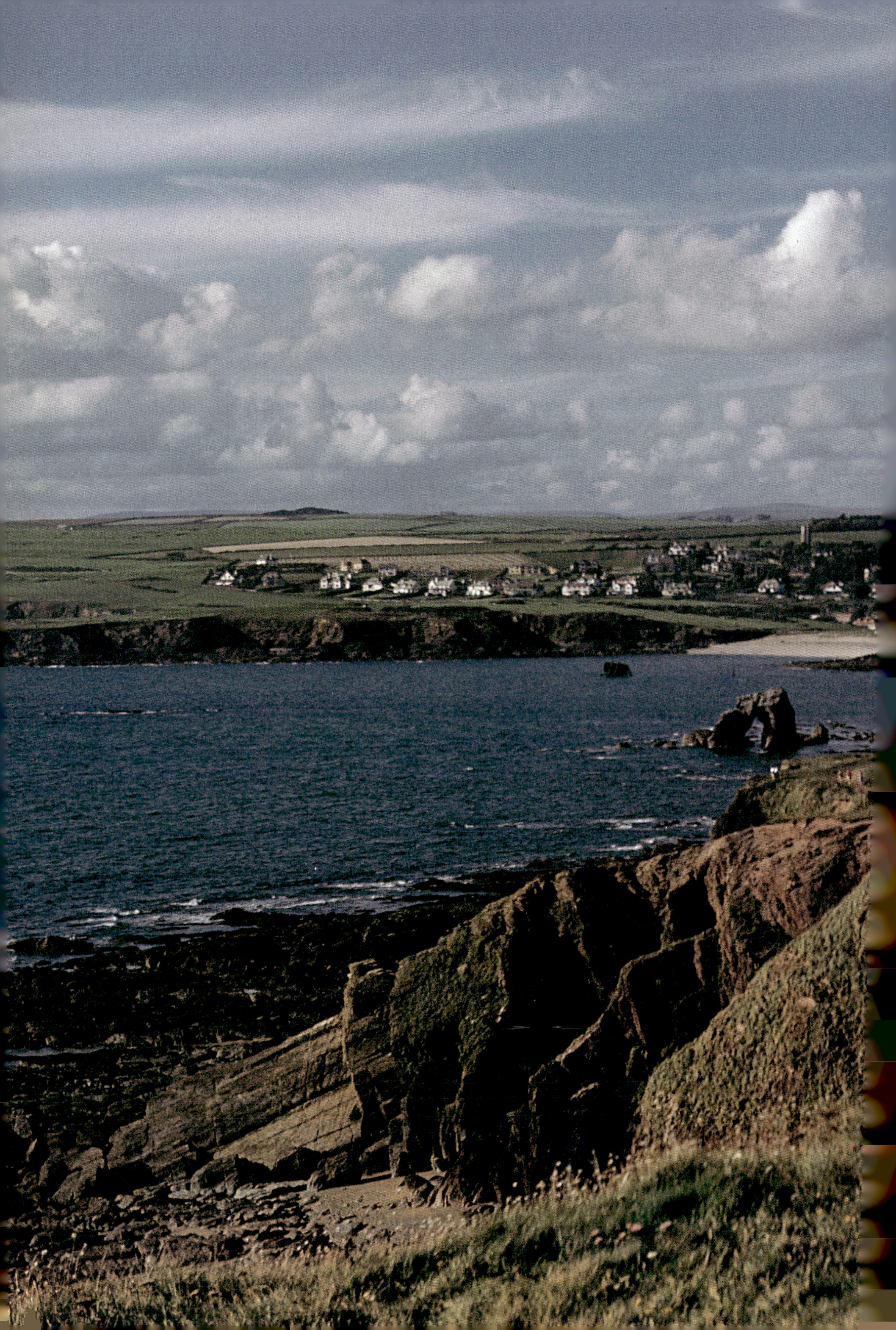

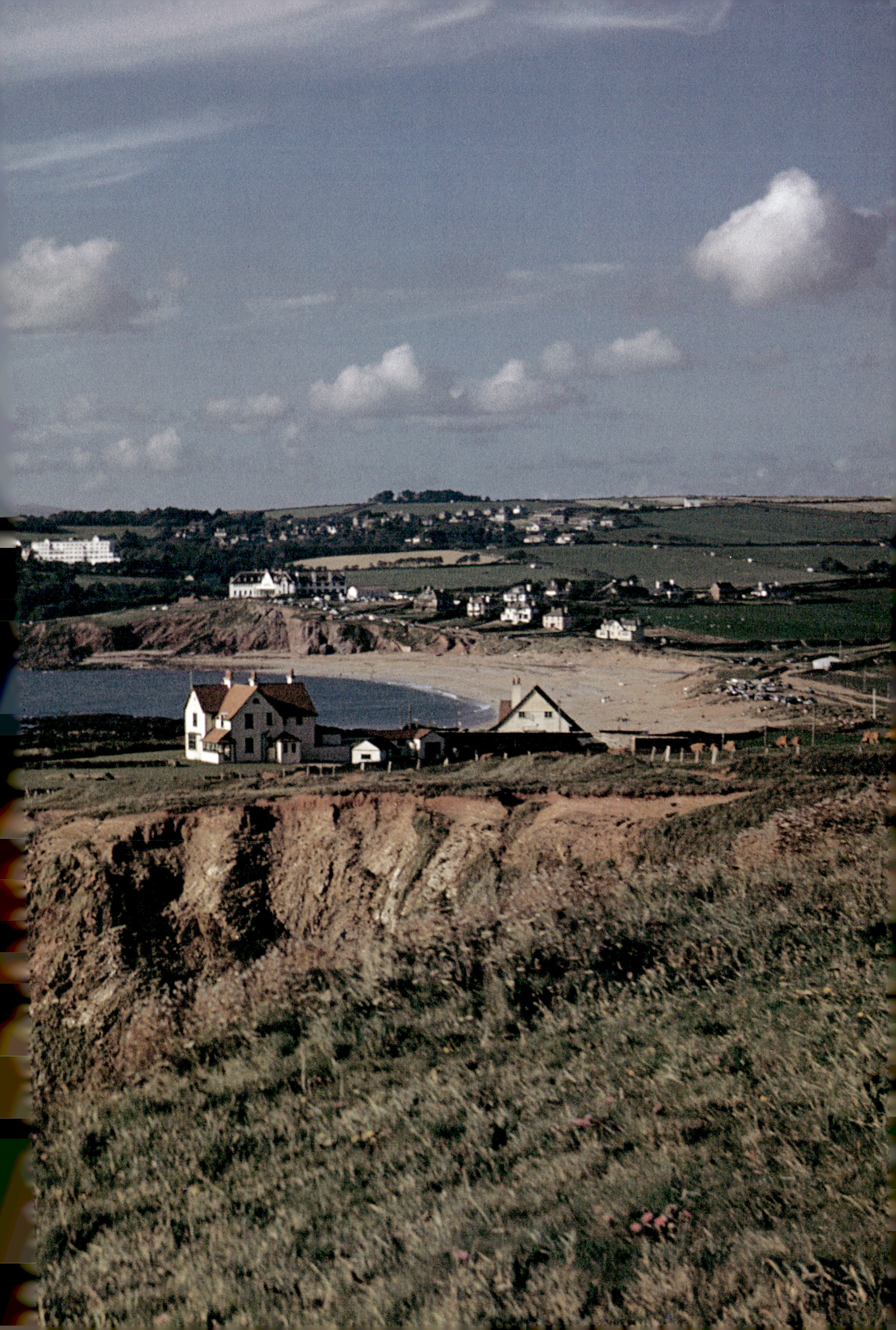

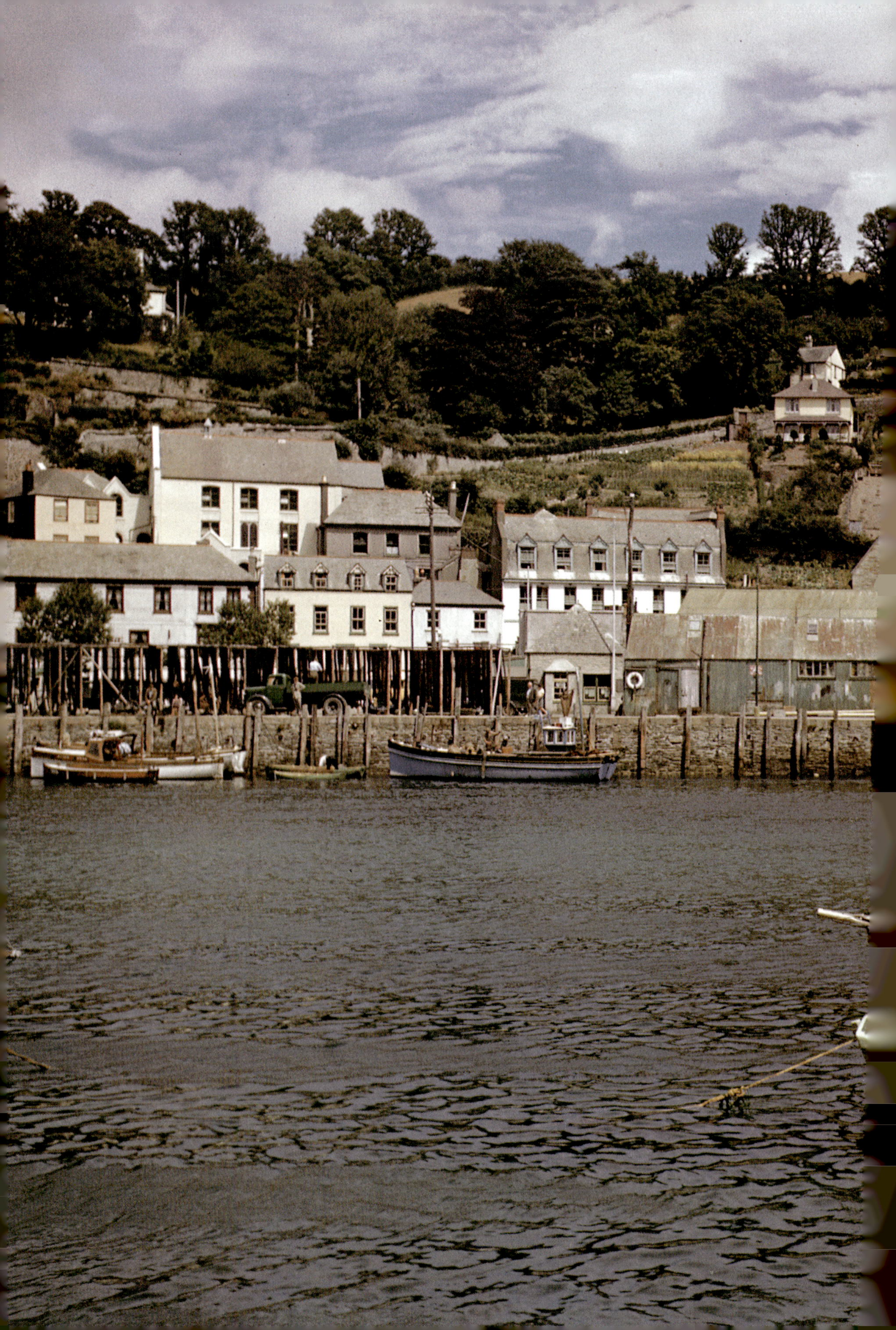

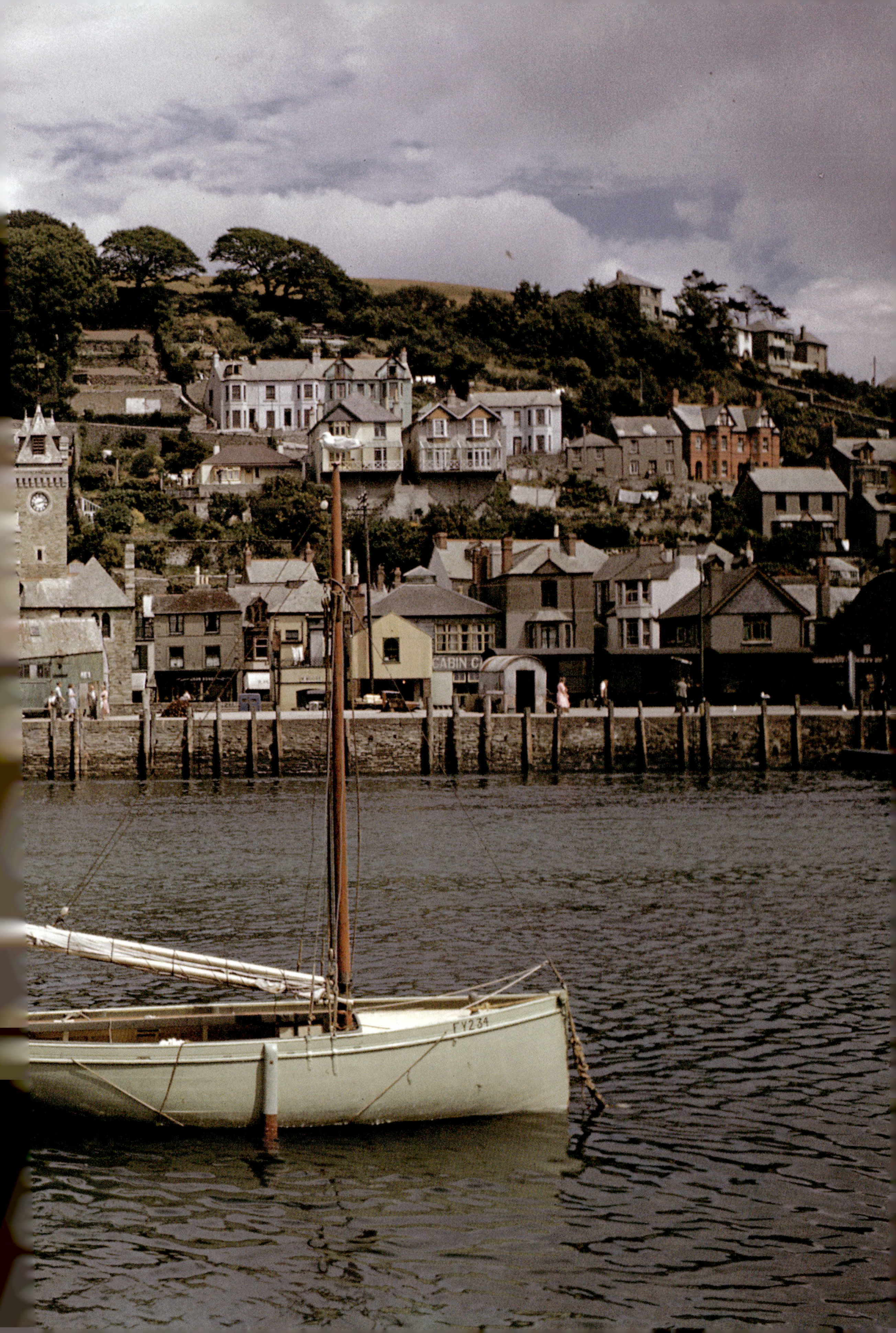
CABIN
FY 234

Polperro

Old fishermen's cottages overlook the little harbour at Polperro, about 3 miles along the Cornish coast from Looe.

Artists' paradise
(overleaf)

Polperro is one of the prettiest places in England, huddled on England's most romantic coast, where the stream, the Pol, flows down a deep valley between rocky headlands, and runs into the sea between the old stone cottages.

Polperro harbour
(overleaf pp 80/81)

Despite all the gift shops and summer visitors, Polperro is still one of the most picturesque of Cornwall's fishing villages.

O THE CLIFF
TURN RIGHT

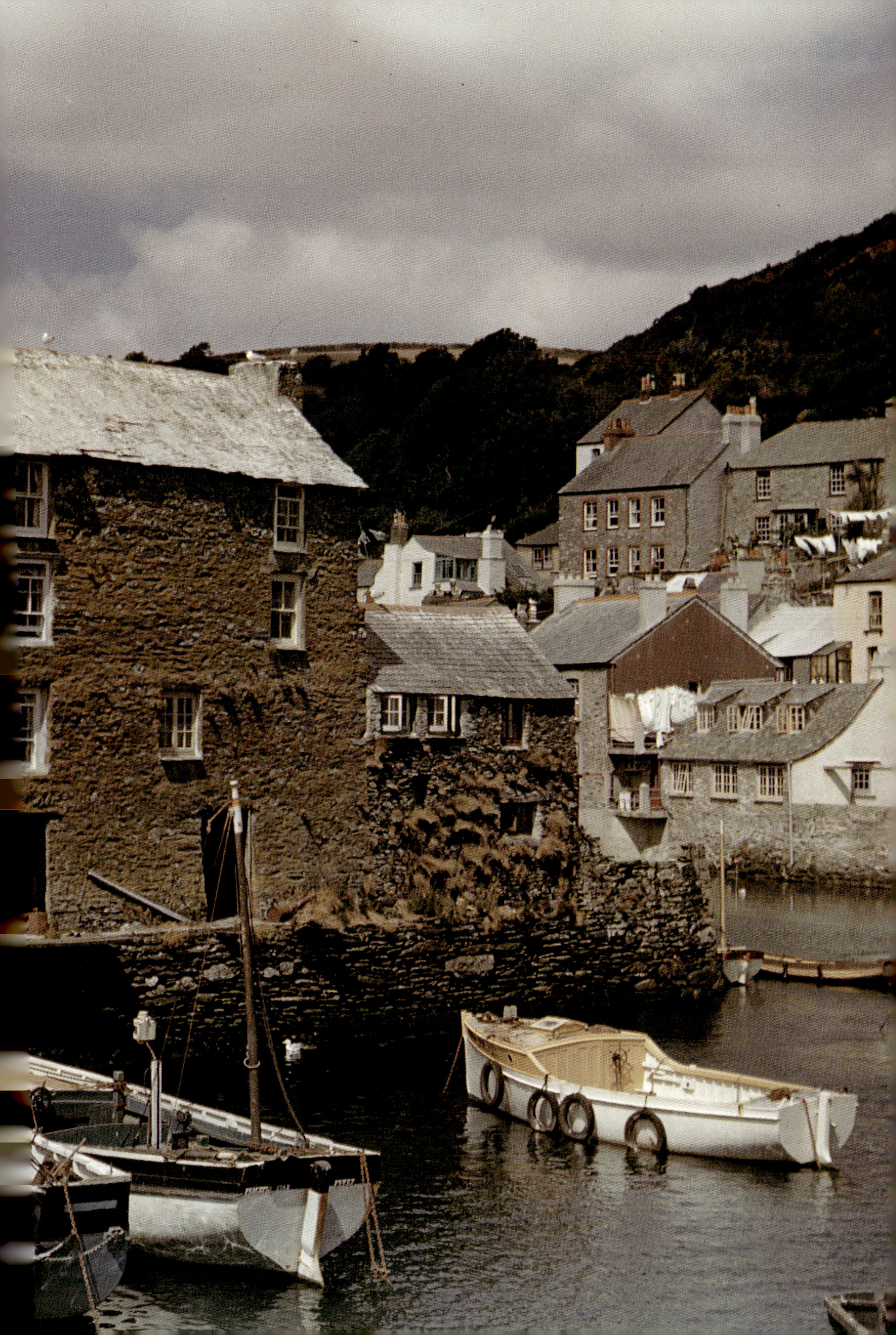

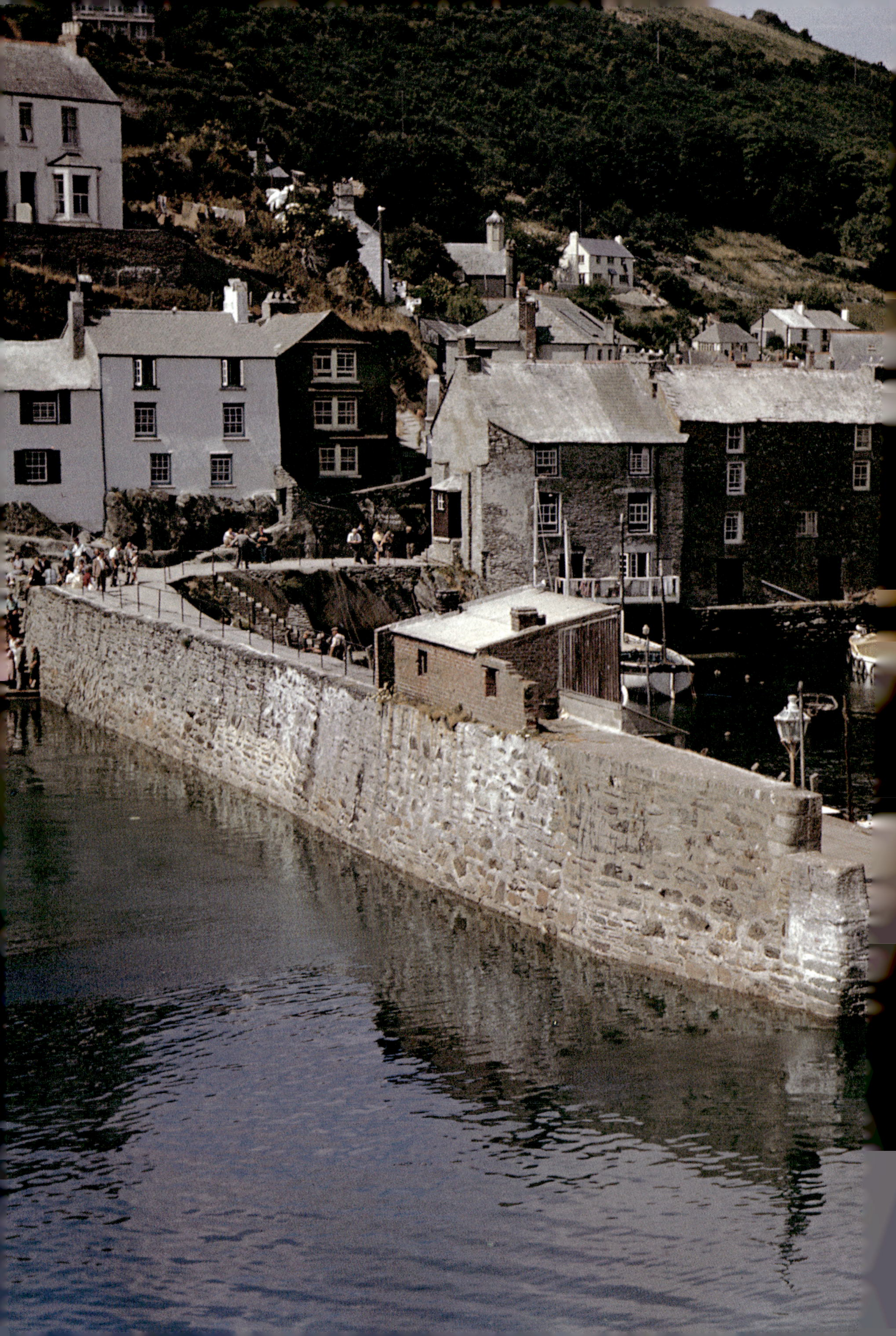

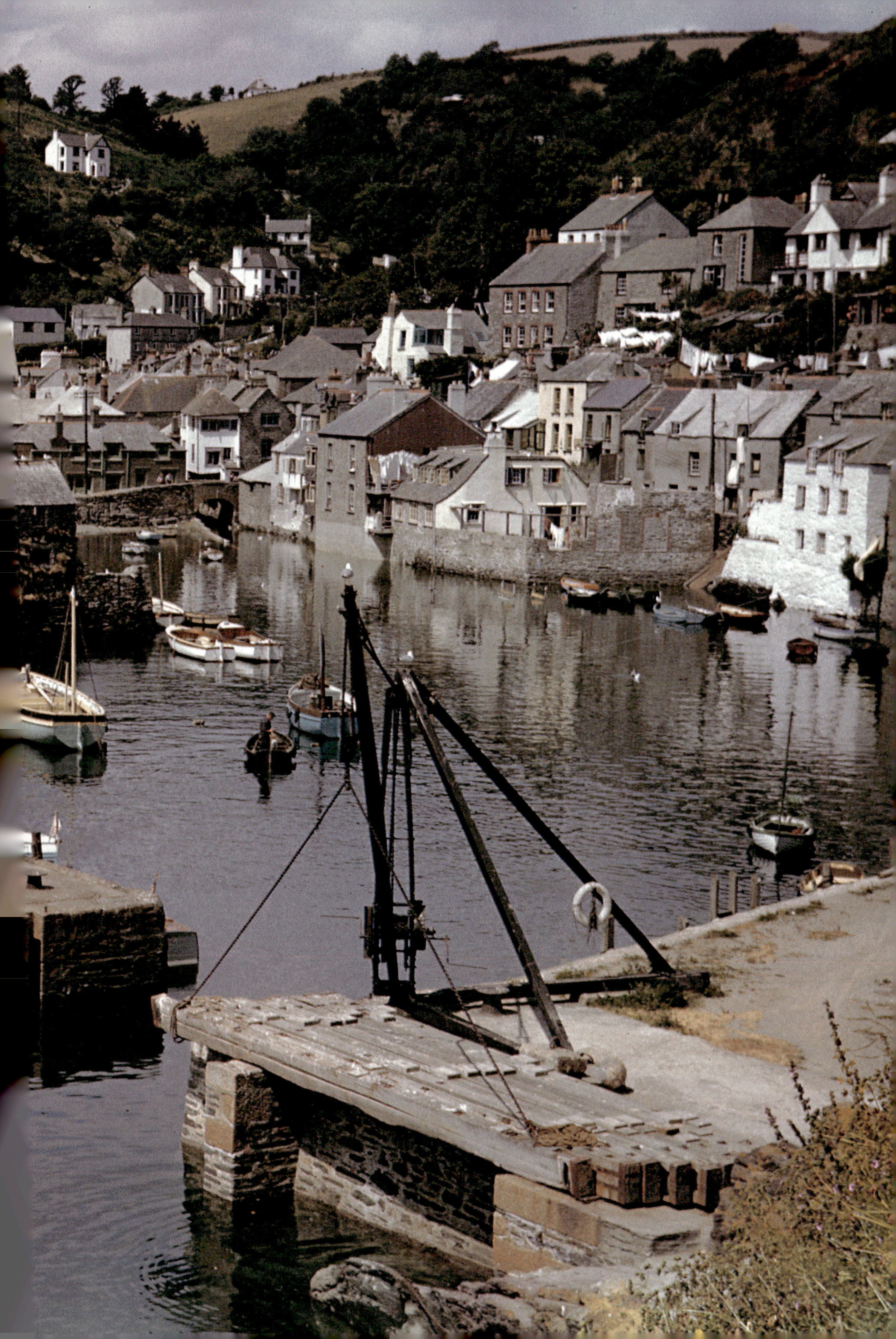

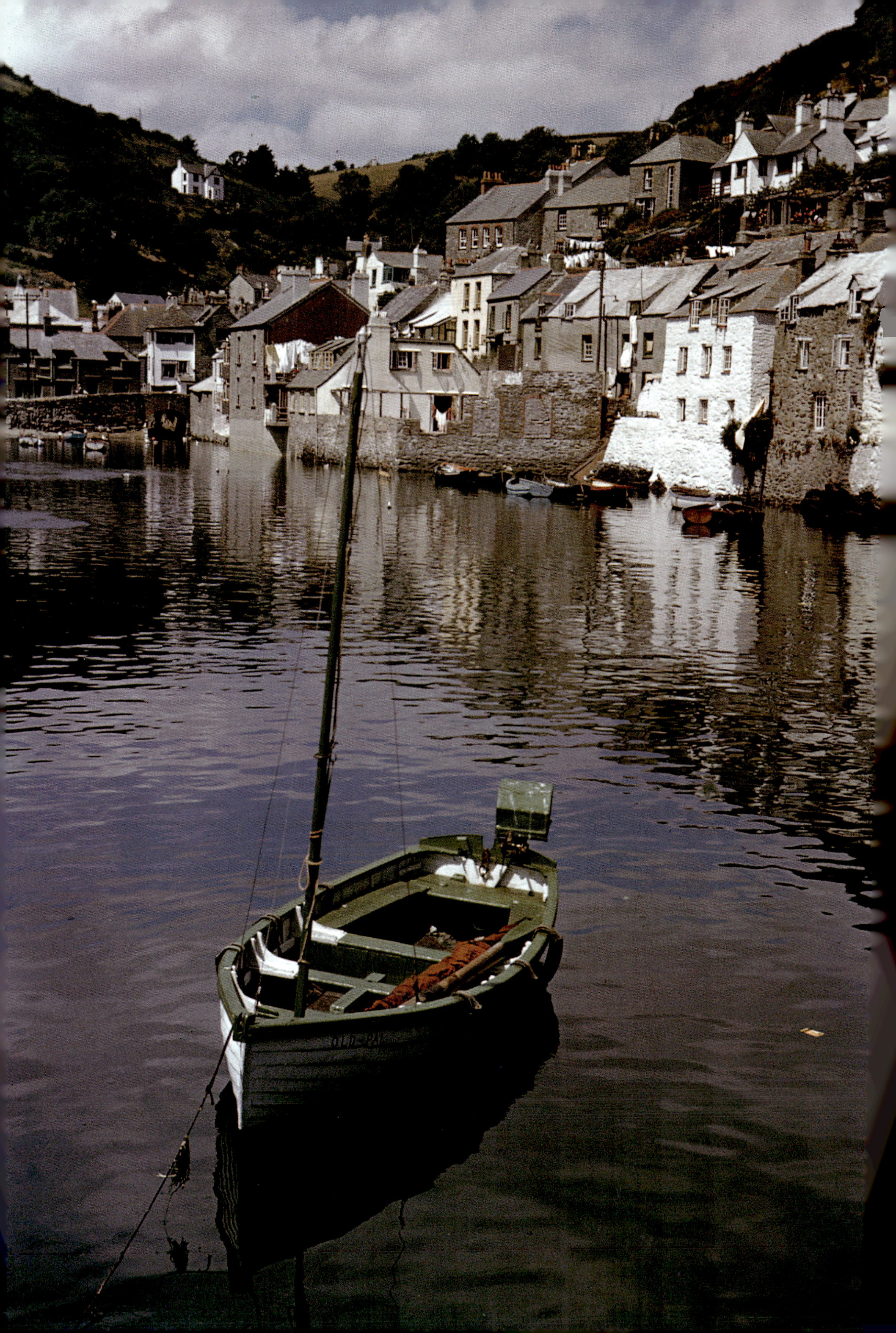

Boat at anchor

The little Cornish harbours are often crowded with boats, and the difficulty is to find a viewpoint that will exclude some of them – for it is the individual craft on the water, backed by a few quaint cottages, that usually provides the best camera study.

Carlyon Bay

This resort near St Austell on Cornwall's south coast is popular with families because of its exceptionally large, quiet beach.

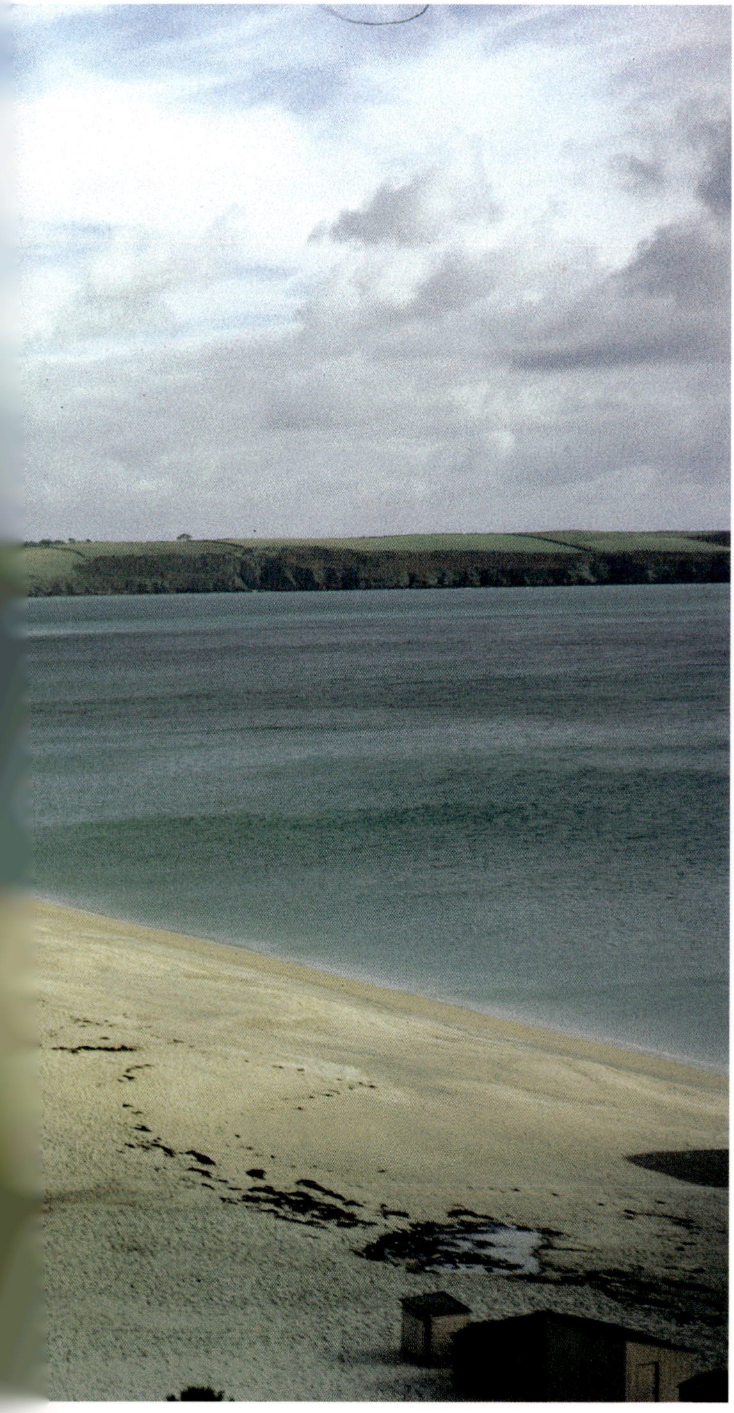

Charlestown

The water in the harbour turns milky-white, for this is one of the main china-clay ports serving St Austell.

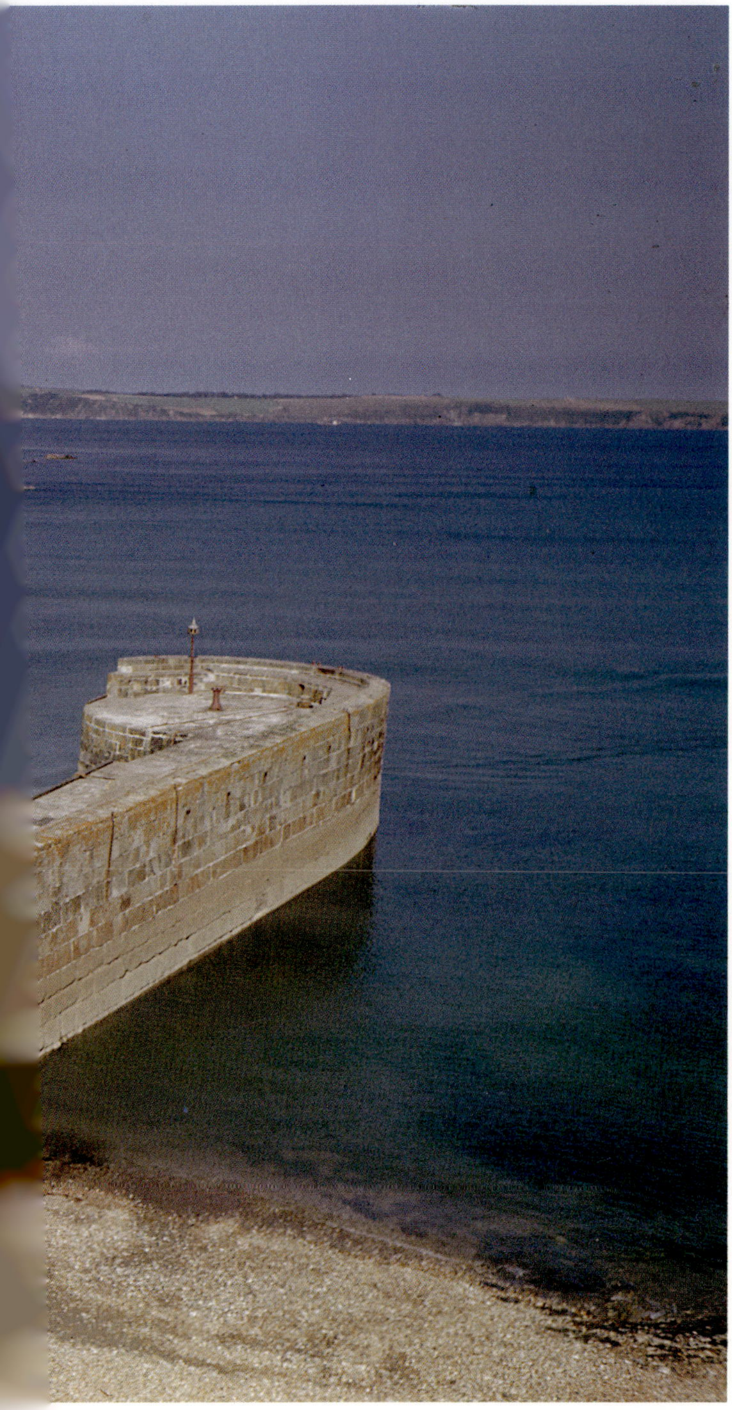

Roche

On the road north from St Austell to Padstow you will find this amazing cluster of huge granite crags, with a ruined chapel built into it at one end (see following picture).

The ruined chapel
(overleaf)

Originally a medieval oratory dedicated to St Michael, Roche has been an object of reverence and curiosity for 600 years. The chapel was built over the cell of a once-celebrated hermit called Conan.

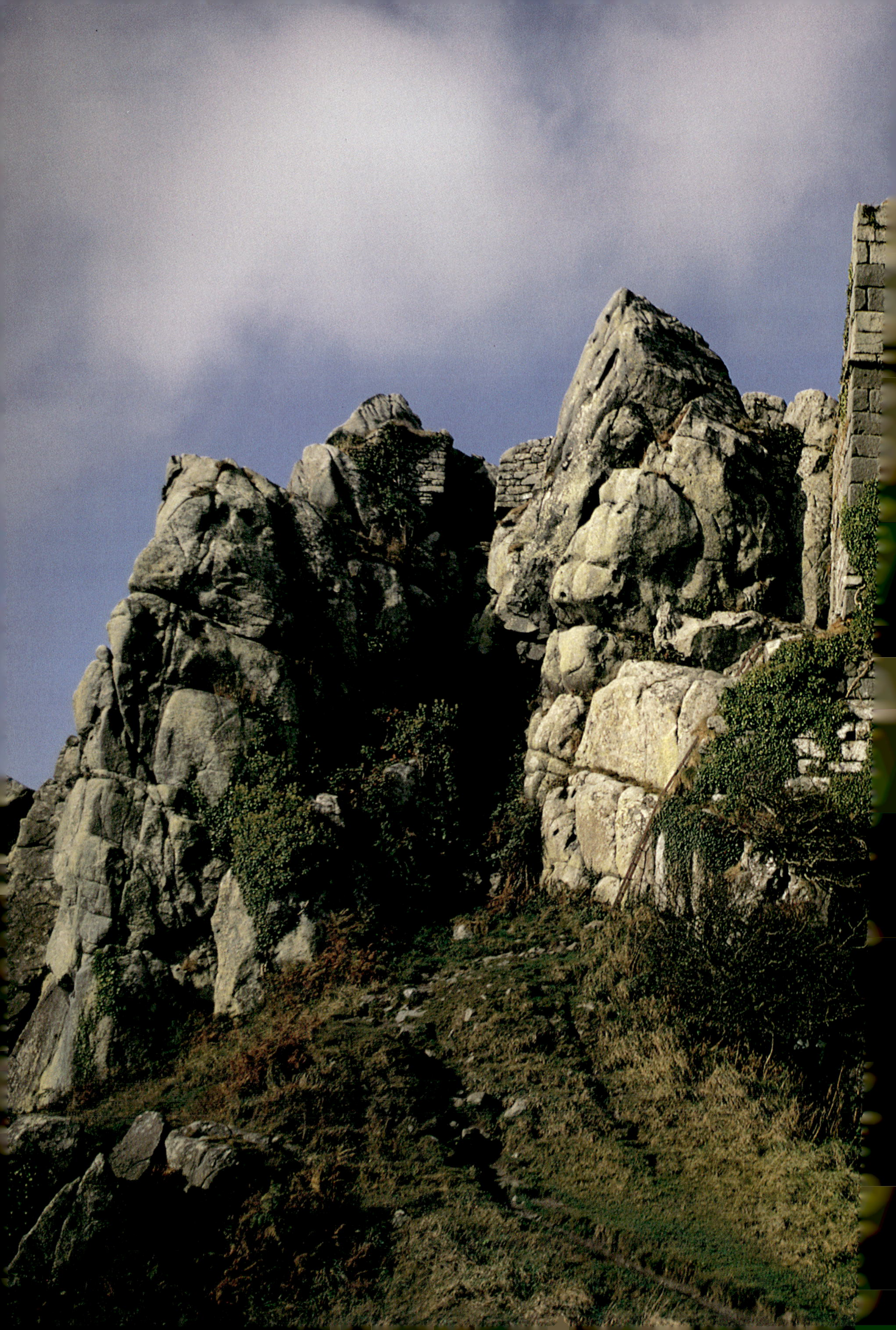

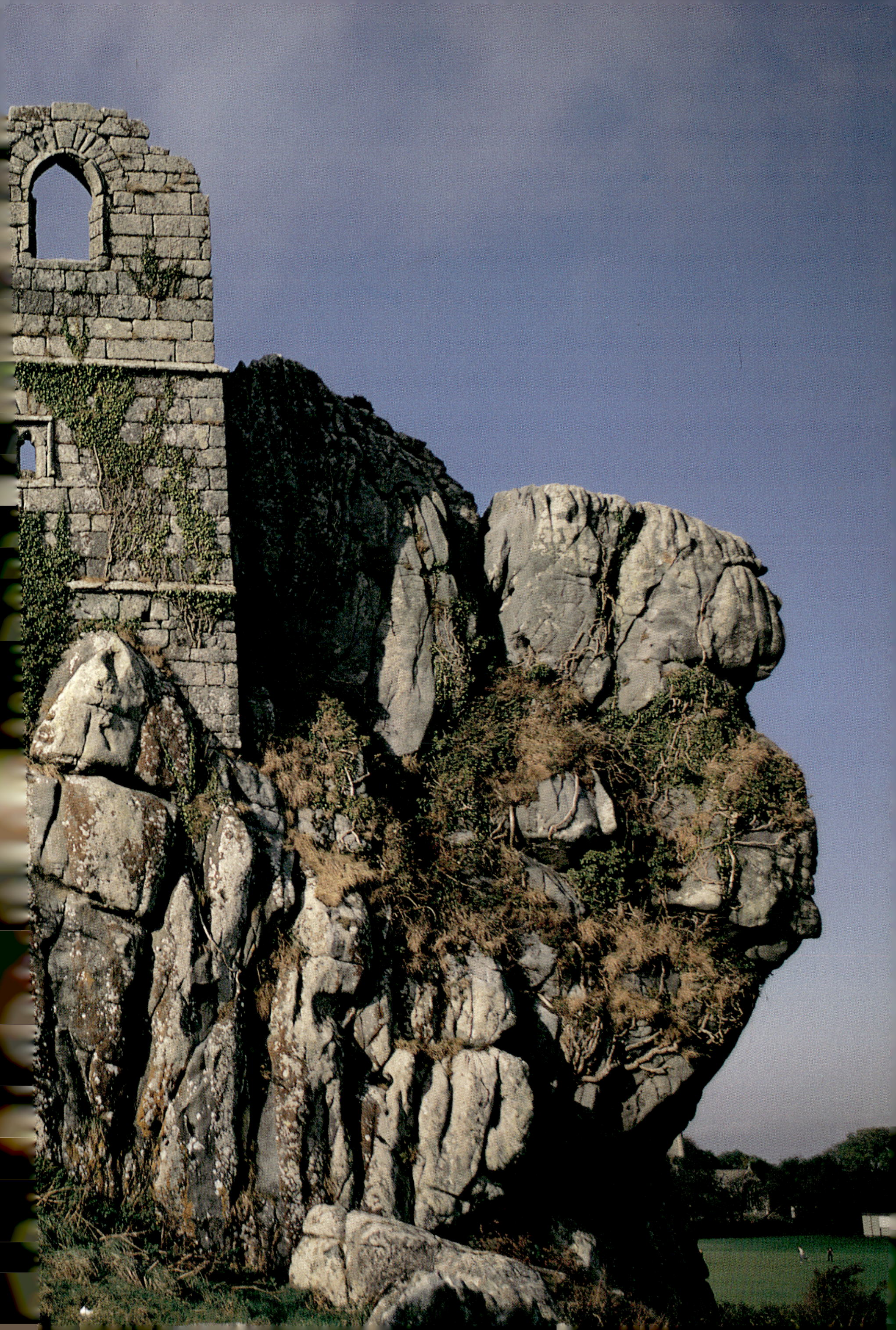

Mevagissey
(here and overleaf)

Once one of the prettiest fishing-ports of Cornwall's south coast, Mevagissey is now sadly overcrowded throughout the summer. It is a centre of the pilchard industry.

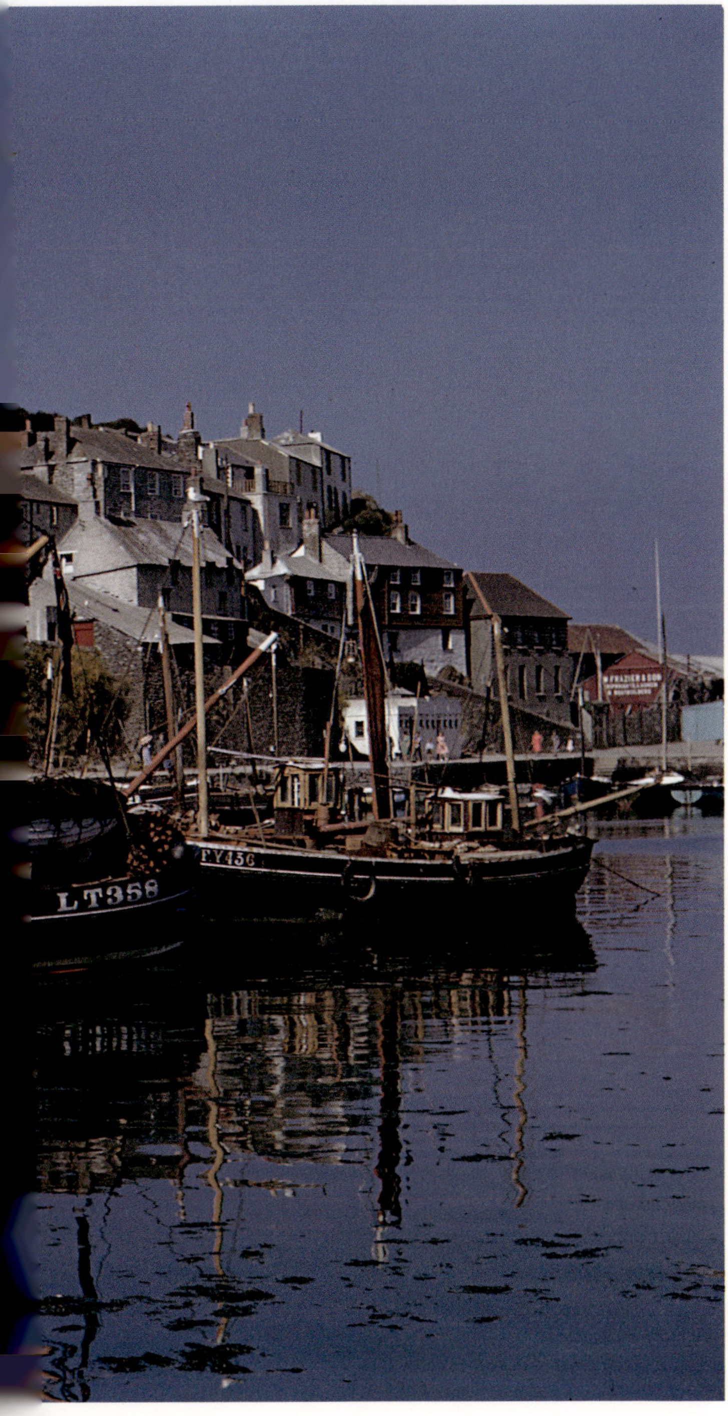
LT358
FY456

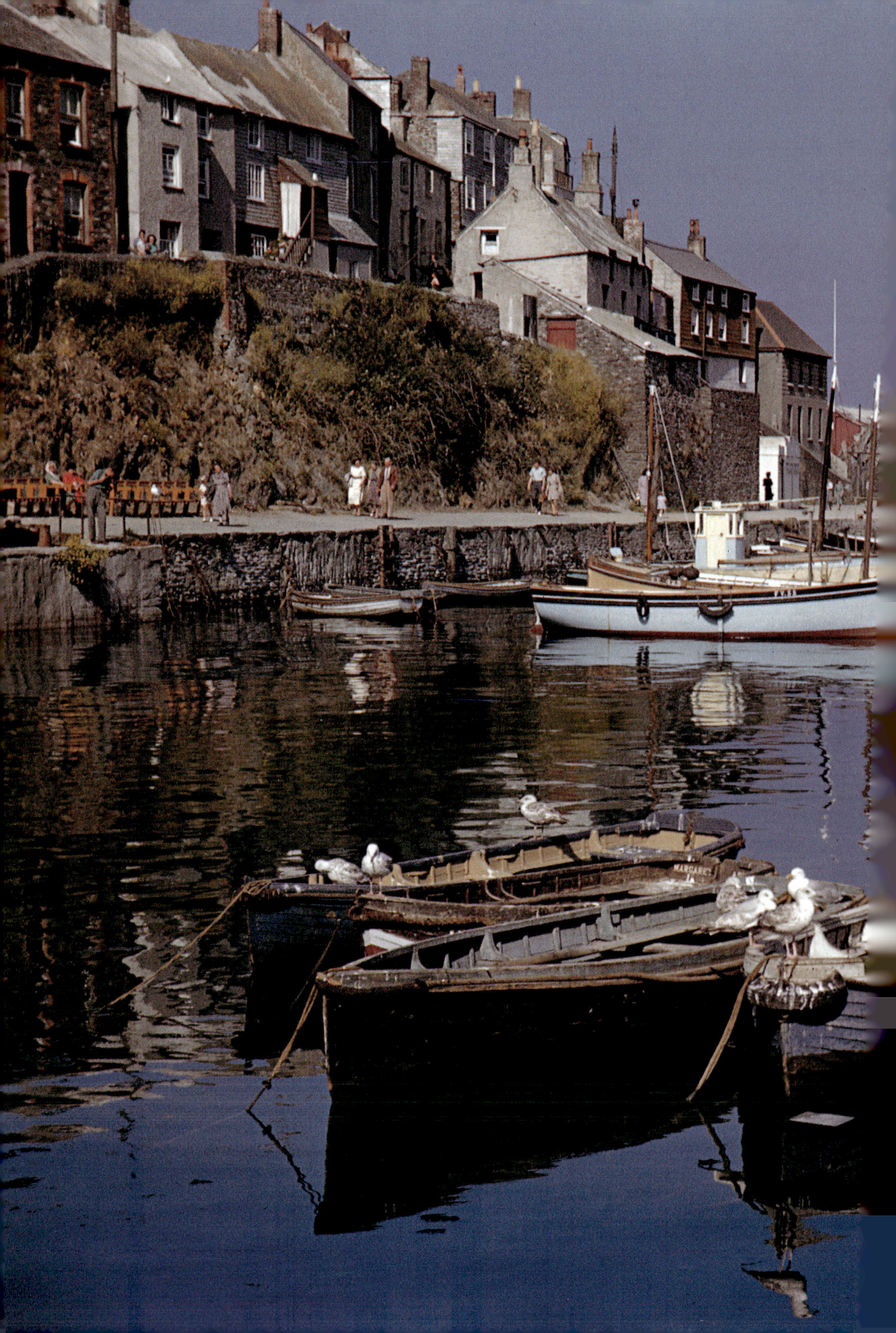

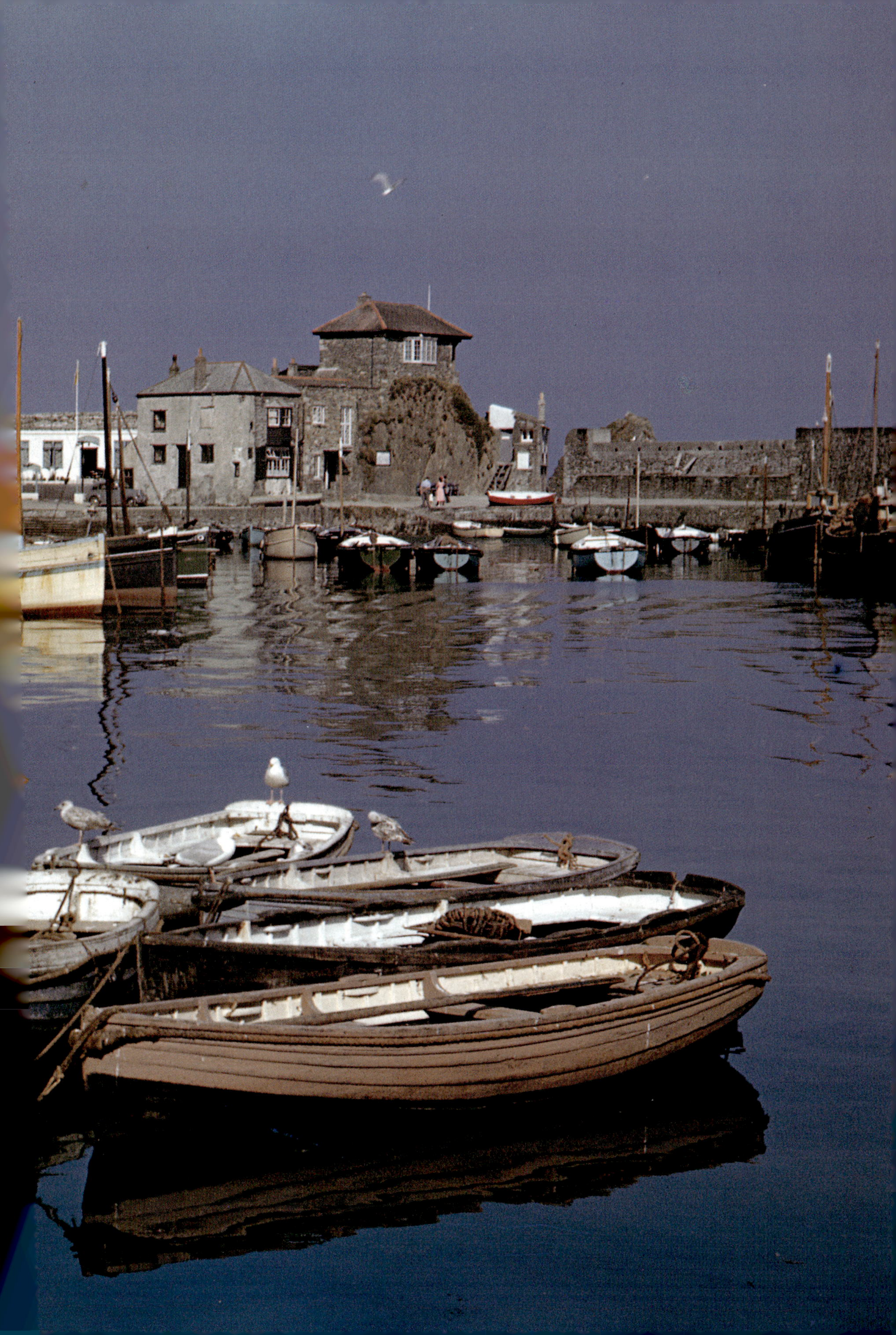

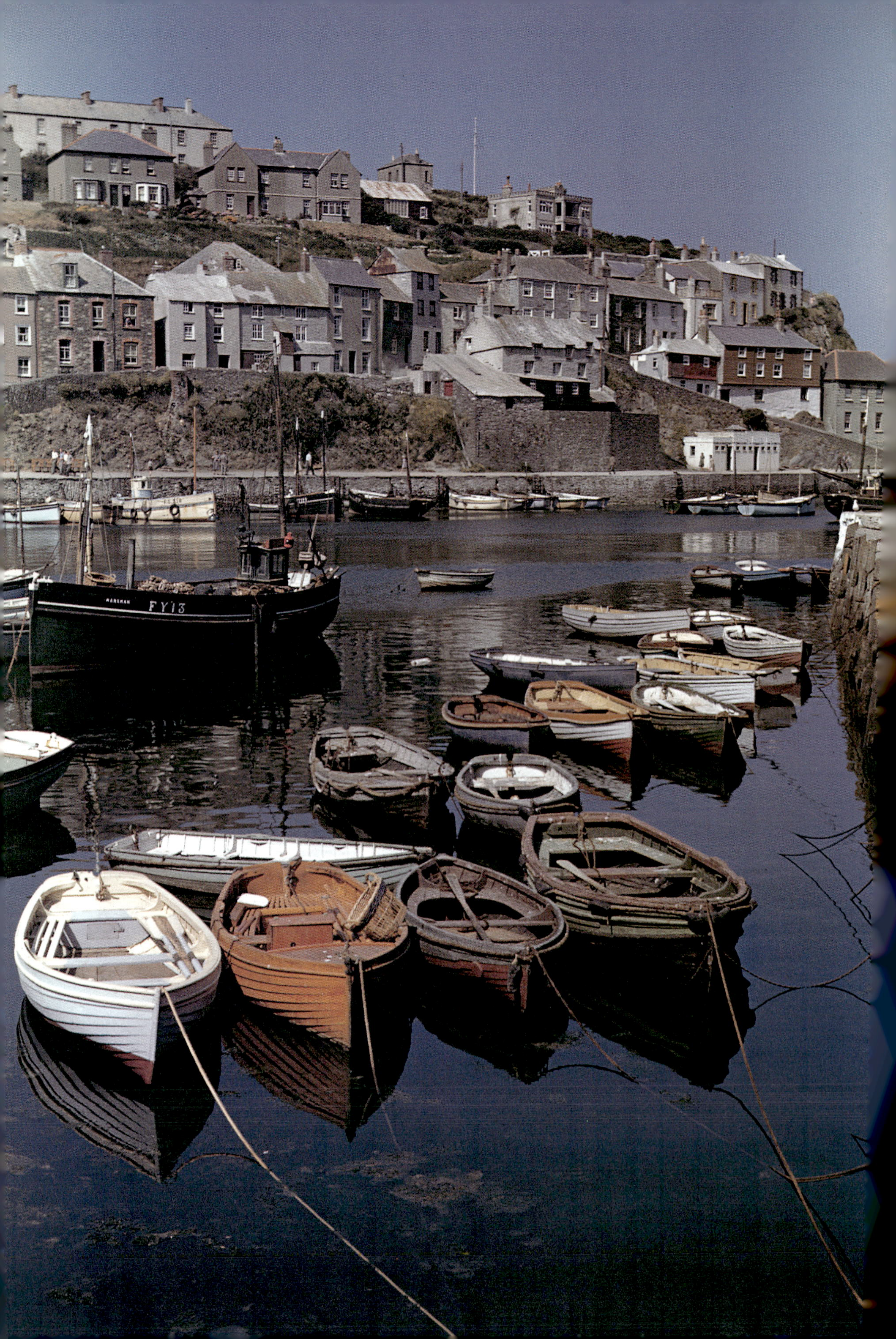
FY13

Still waters

Photographers in the little harbours of the West Country need calm weather if they are to capture reflections at their best – as seen in this picture taken at Mevagissey.

The Lizard

This is the most southerly tip of England: a promontory jutting out into the Channel, its jagged cliffs rising 180 ft above the sea.

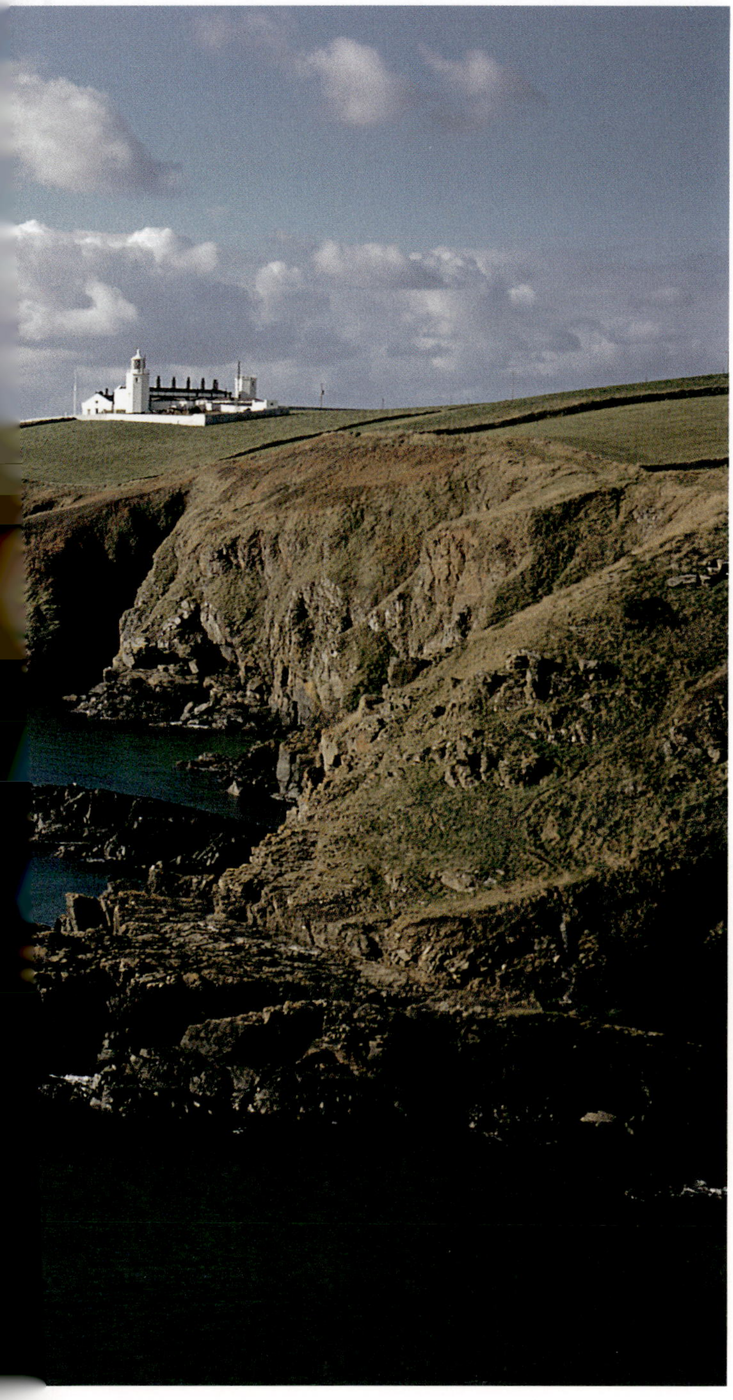

Sun-drenched cliffs

The calm blue sea seen in this picture is deceptive: all around Lizard Point sharp rocks are a danger to shipping, and a succession of lighthouses has been built here since the seventeenth century, when a coal fire was kept burning on the cliffs.

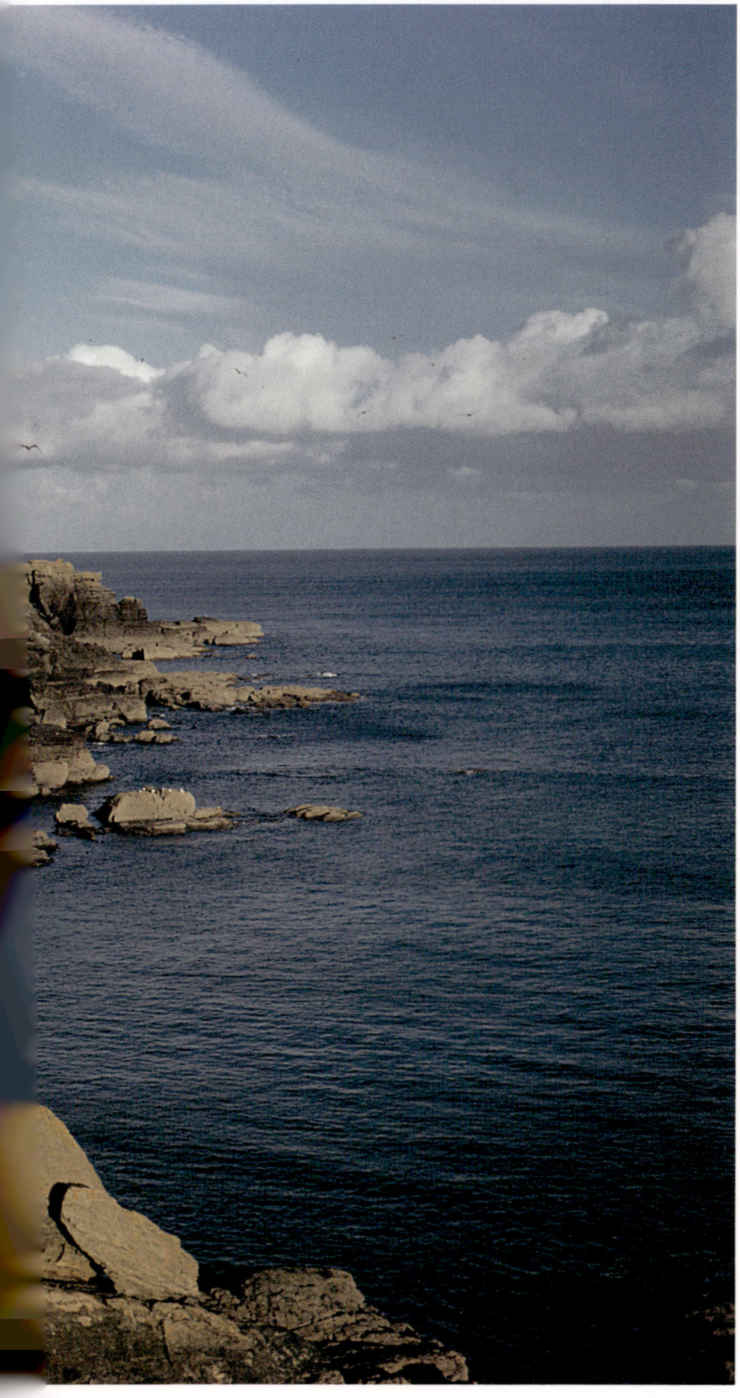

A Cornish hamlet

This little group of whitewashed houses nestles in a fold of the cliffs near the Lizard.

Sandy bay near Kynance Cove
(overleaf)

The Cornish coast may be crowded in summer, but there are still many secluded coves such as this, where you can enjoy a solitary hour or two at low tide. But the swiftness of the incoming sea can easily trap the unwary.

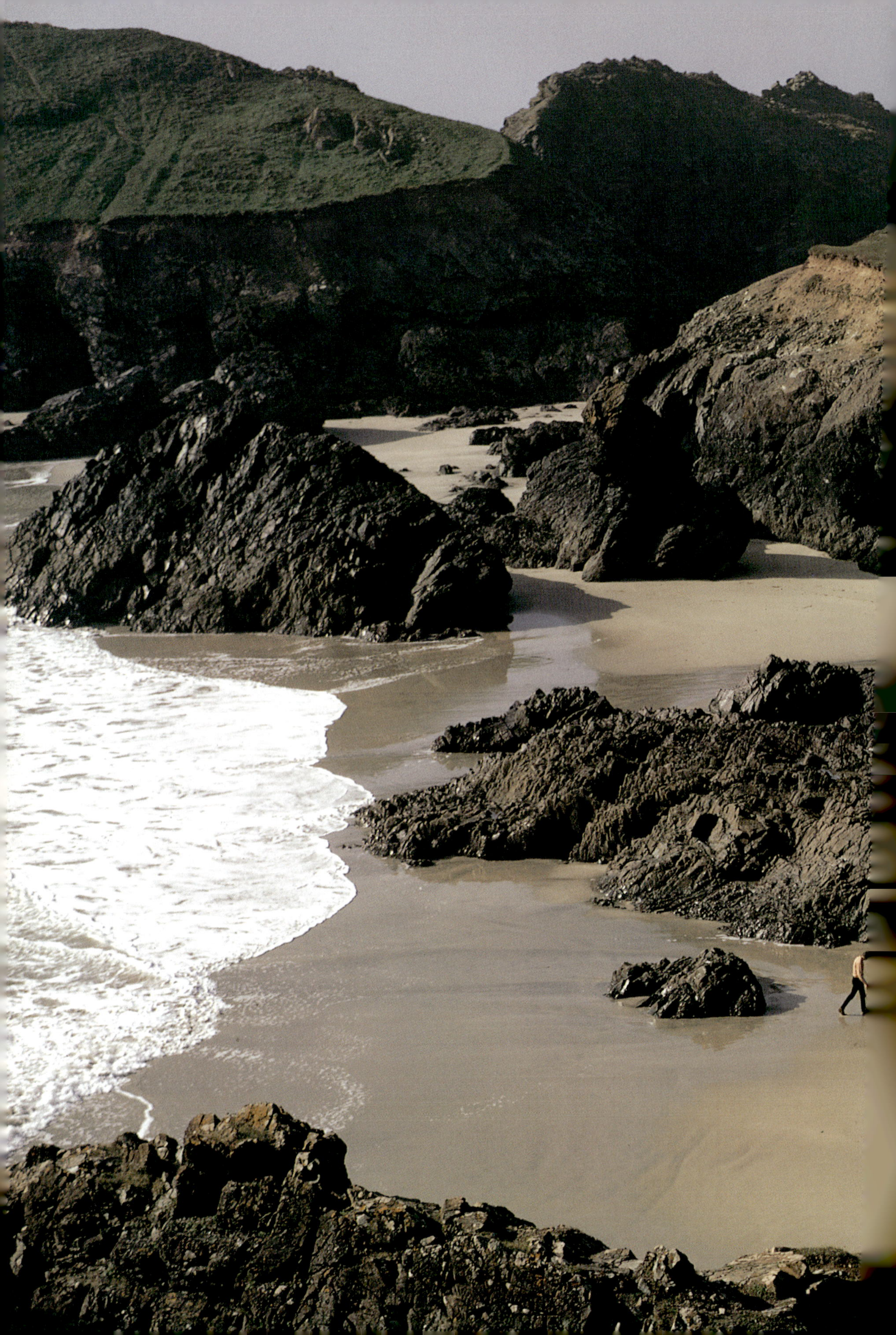

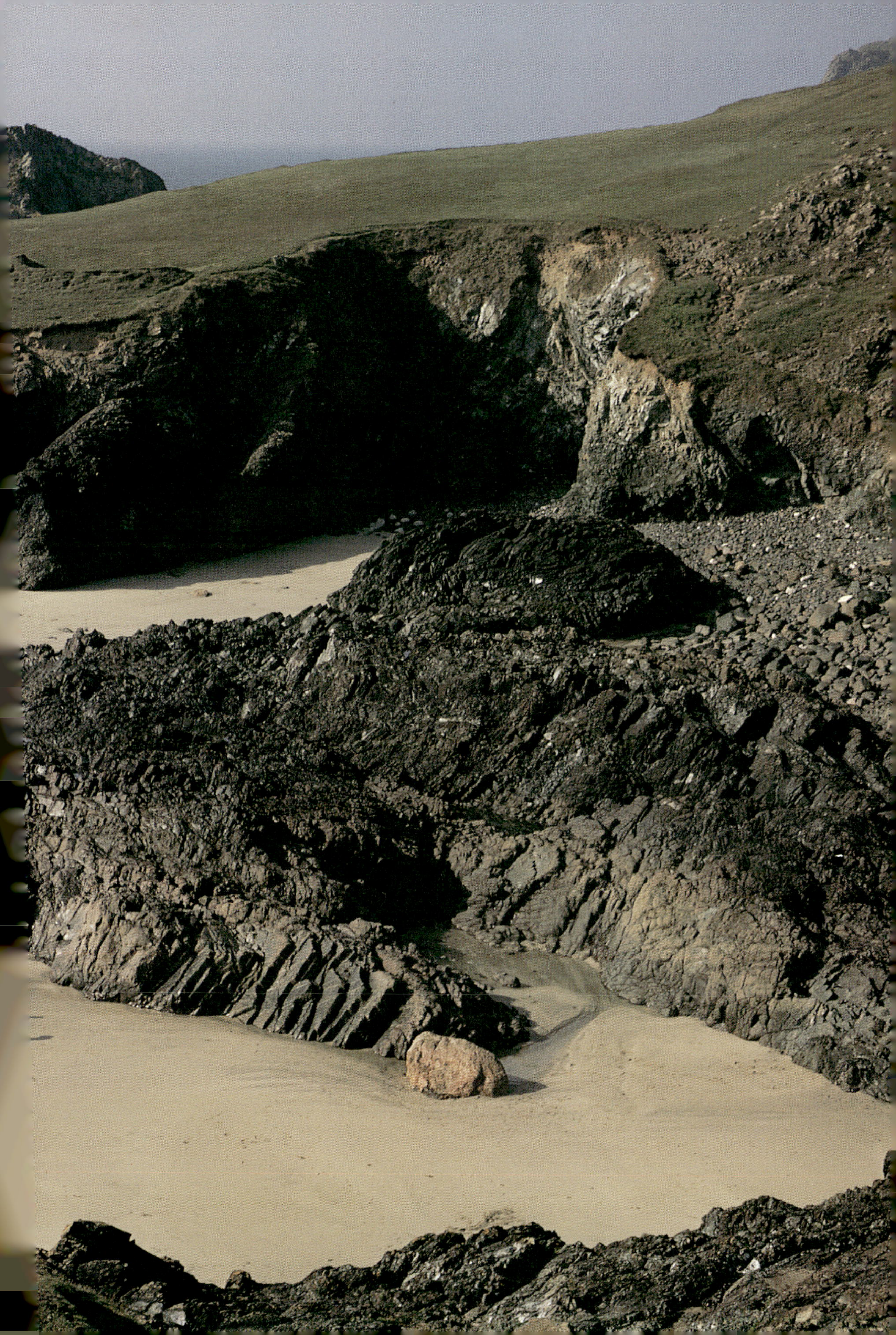

Kynance Cove

This is one of the most magnificent inlets on the
Cornish coast and is best seen, as in this picture,
from the cliffs to the south.

Rough seas
(overleaf)

Kynance Cove in more tempestuous mood – winds and high seas impart a greater grandeur to the subject.

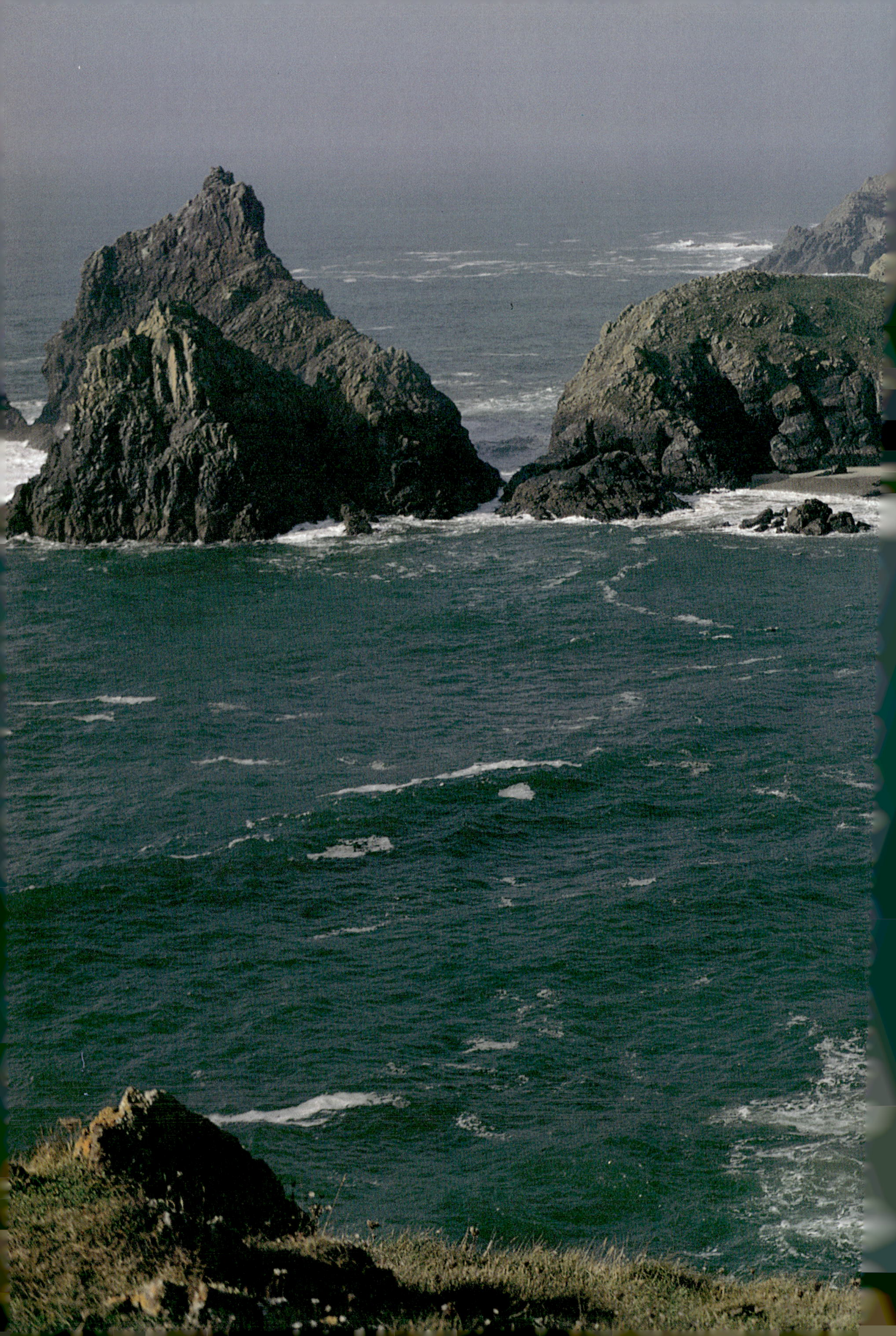

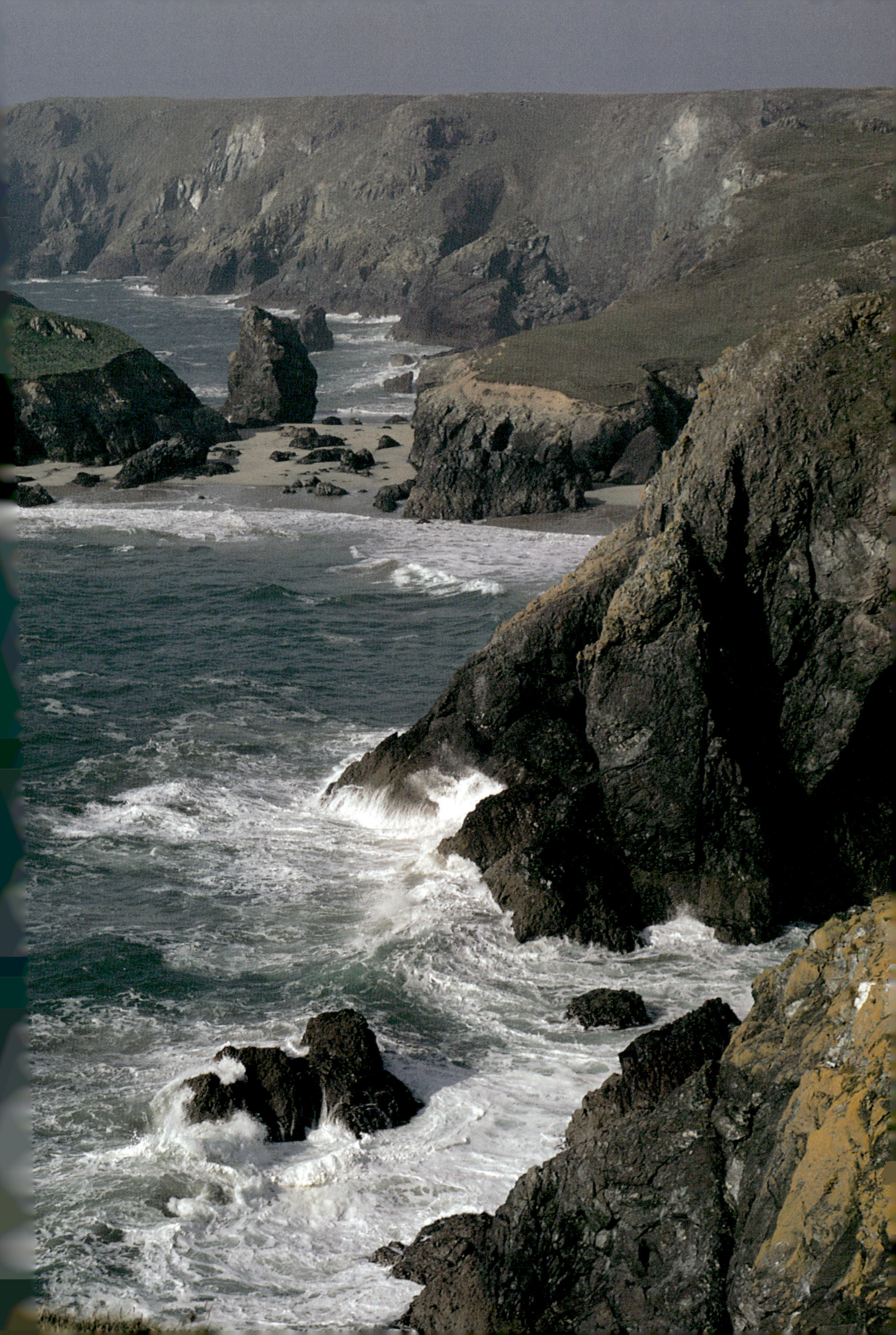

Mullion Cove and harbour

Mullion Cove, now part of the National Trust, boasts a fine cavern and the striking Lion Rock jutting out to sea.

Sunset over Mullion Cove

(overleaf)

The cameraman needs patience and luck to capture the light on water and cloud-masses at its best.

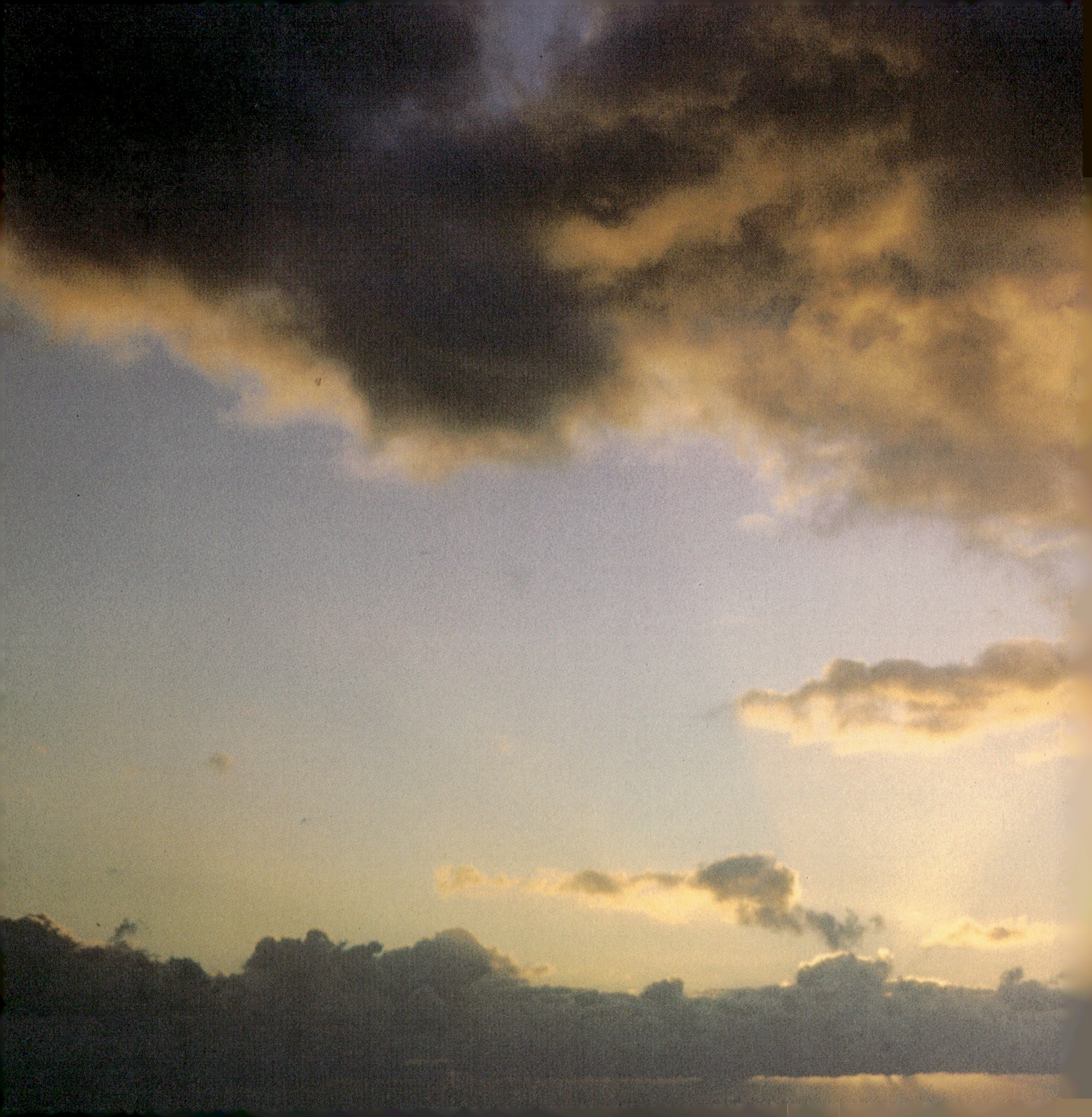

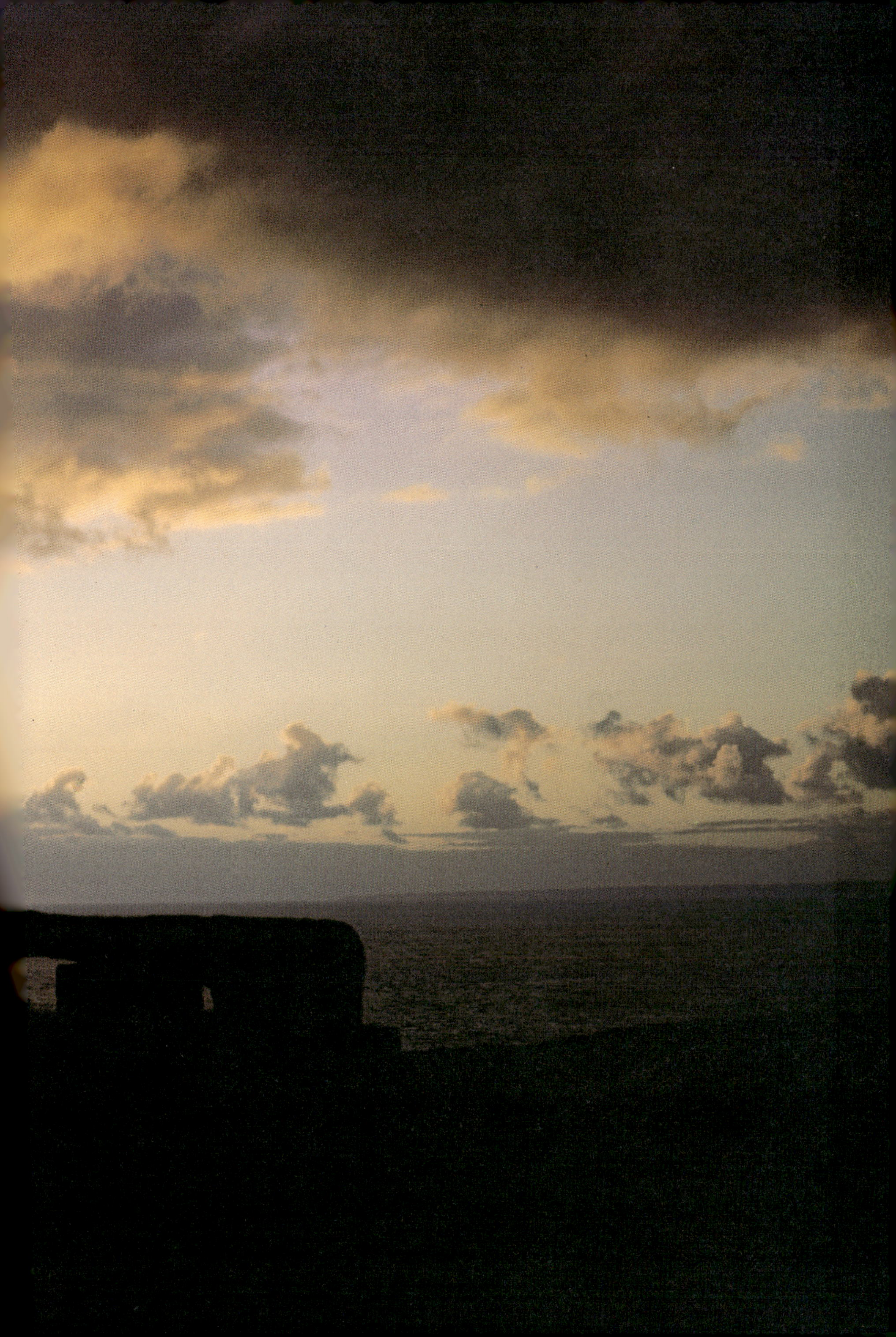

St Michael's Mount

Lying off the coast of Marazion, this was probably once the port of the Phoenician fleet which visited Cornwall 2,500 years ago to barter tin. A monastery and castle, dating from medieval times, now stand there.

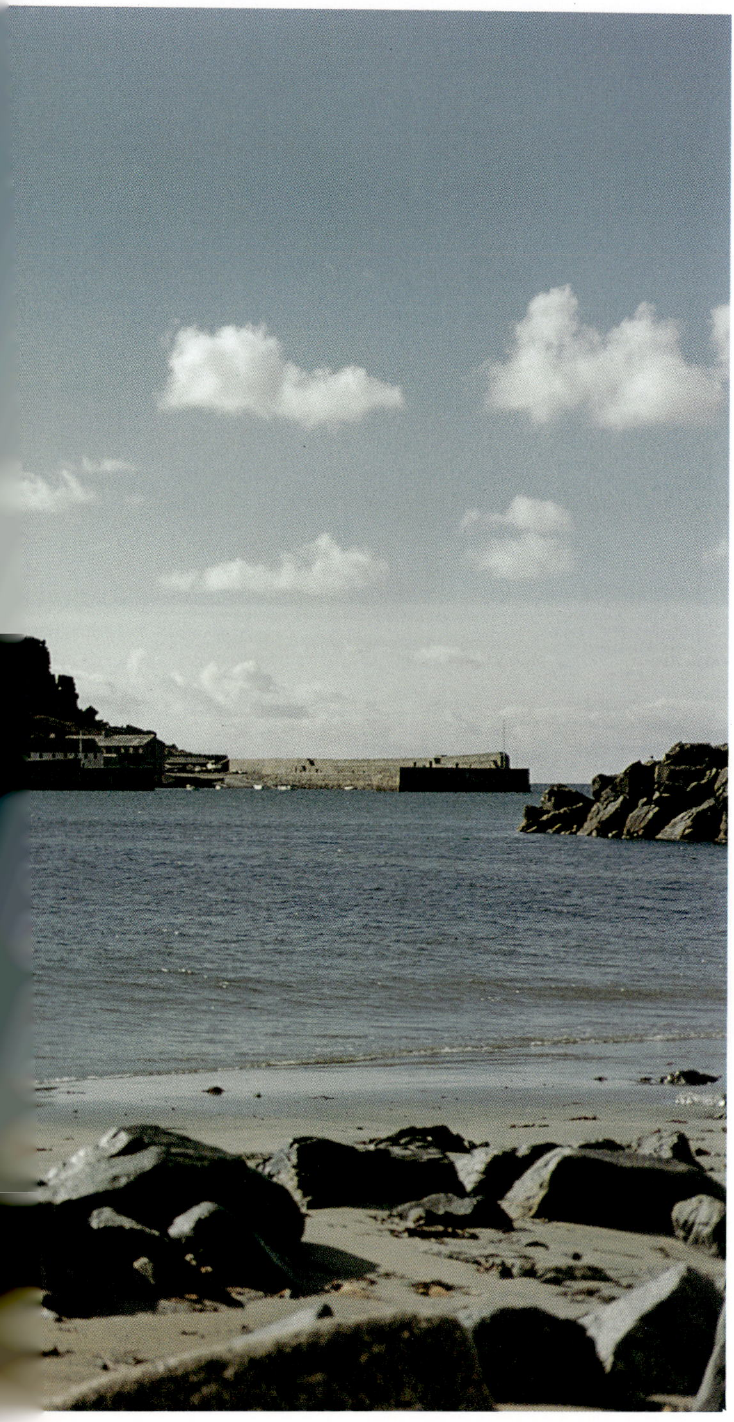

Newlyn

This study shows the old horseshoe harbour, with the fish-market in the background. Newlyn is famous today for its colony of artists.

Mousehole harbour
(overleaf)

Fishing nets hang out to dry in the sun and sea-breezes at Mousehole.

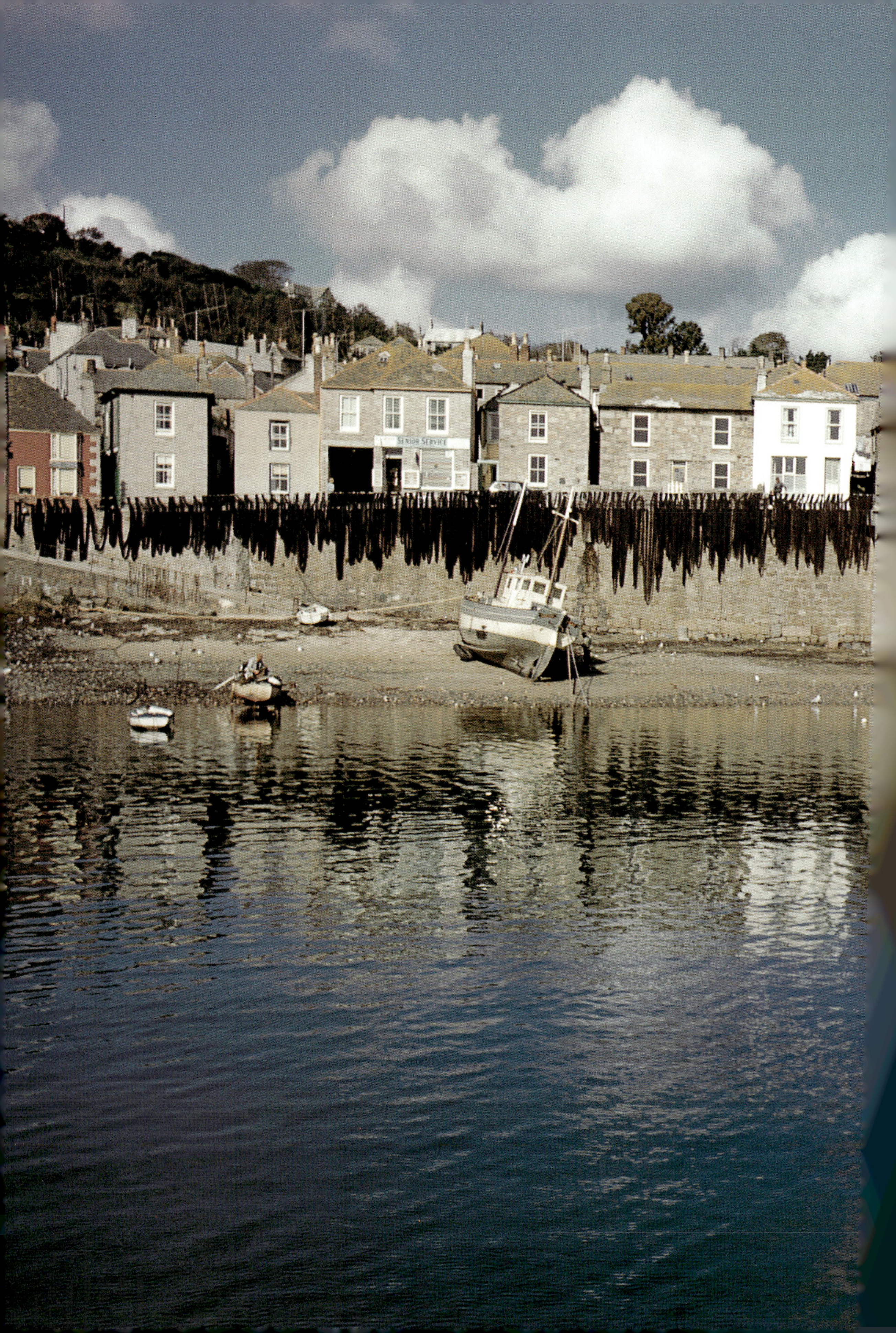
SENIOR SERVICE

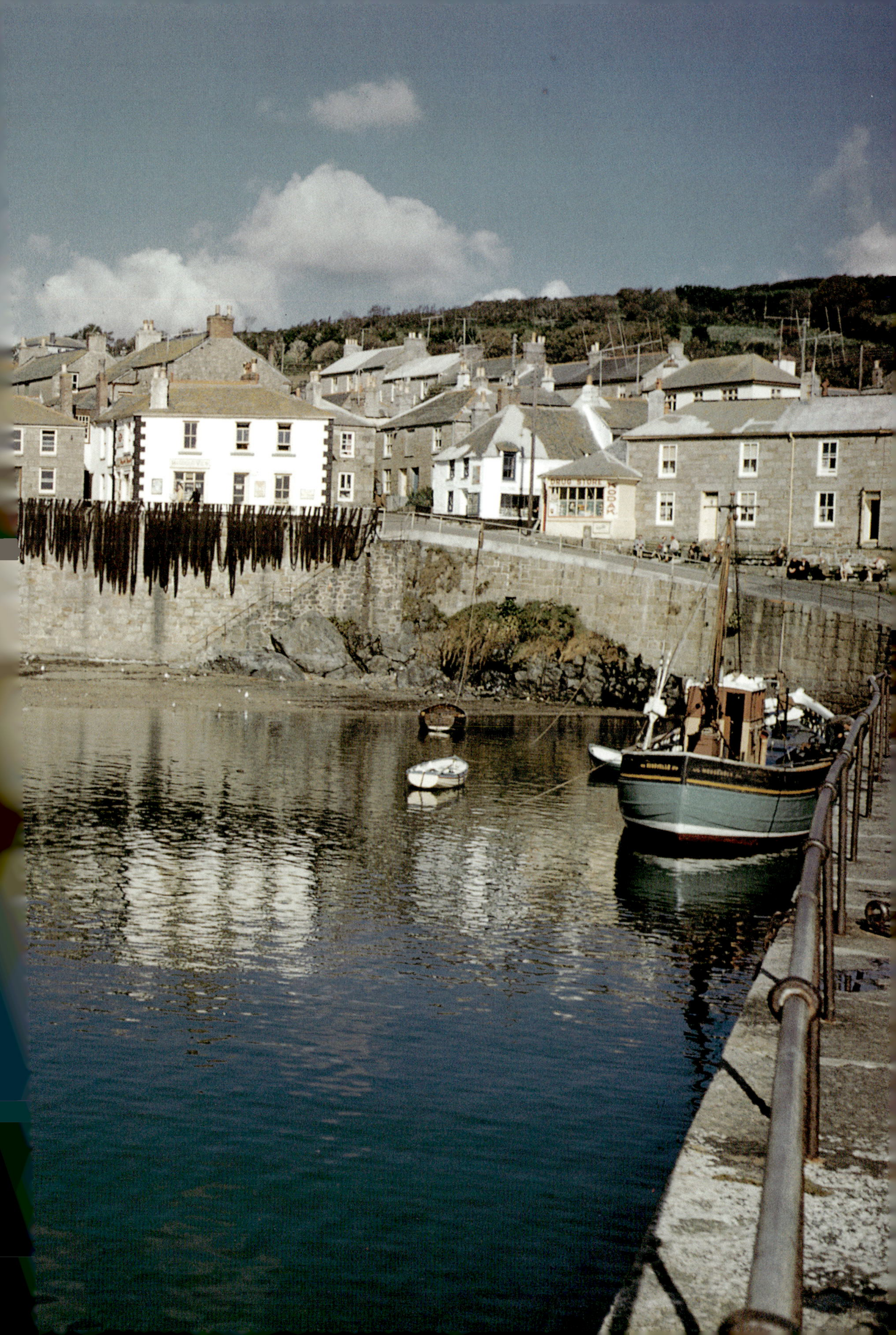

Lamorna Cove and granite quarry

The valley behind Lamorna Cove is exceptionally beautiful, with its combination of steep brackened hillsides and woods.

121

Porthcurno beach

The grand and rocky coast stretching from Penzance to Sennen is broken by Porthcurno's shining sands. They are seen in the distance in this picture, which was taken from the Logan Rock, near Treen.

The Logan Rock in daylight

(overleaf)

The Logan Rock, which can just be seen in this photograph on the summit of the furthest headland, is a block of granite weighing about 60 tons. It was at one time poised so delicately that a touch, it was said, could set it rocking.

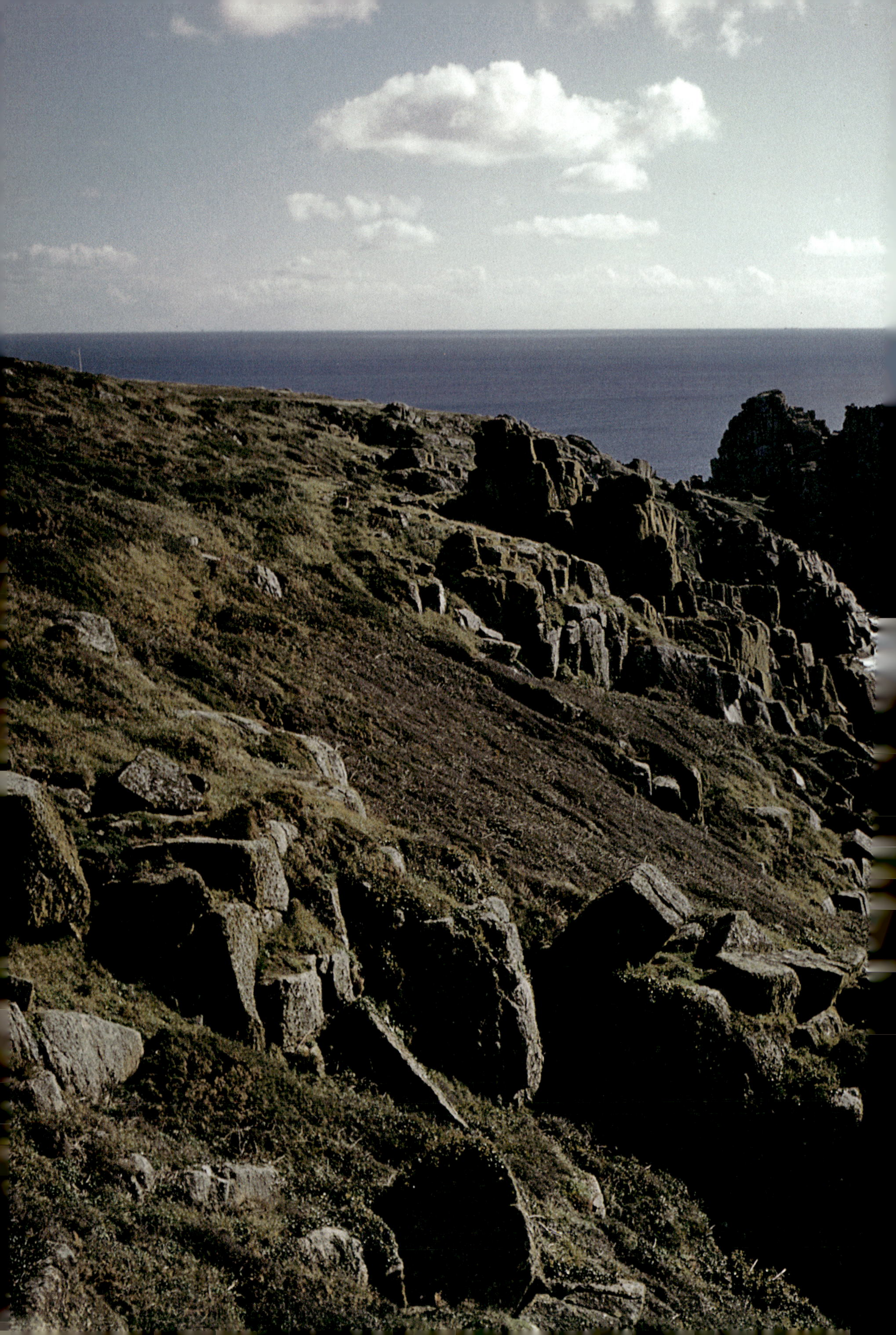

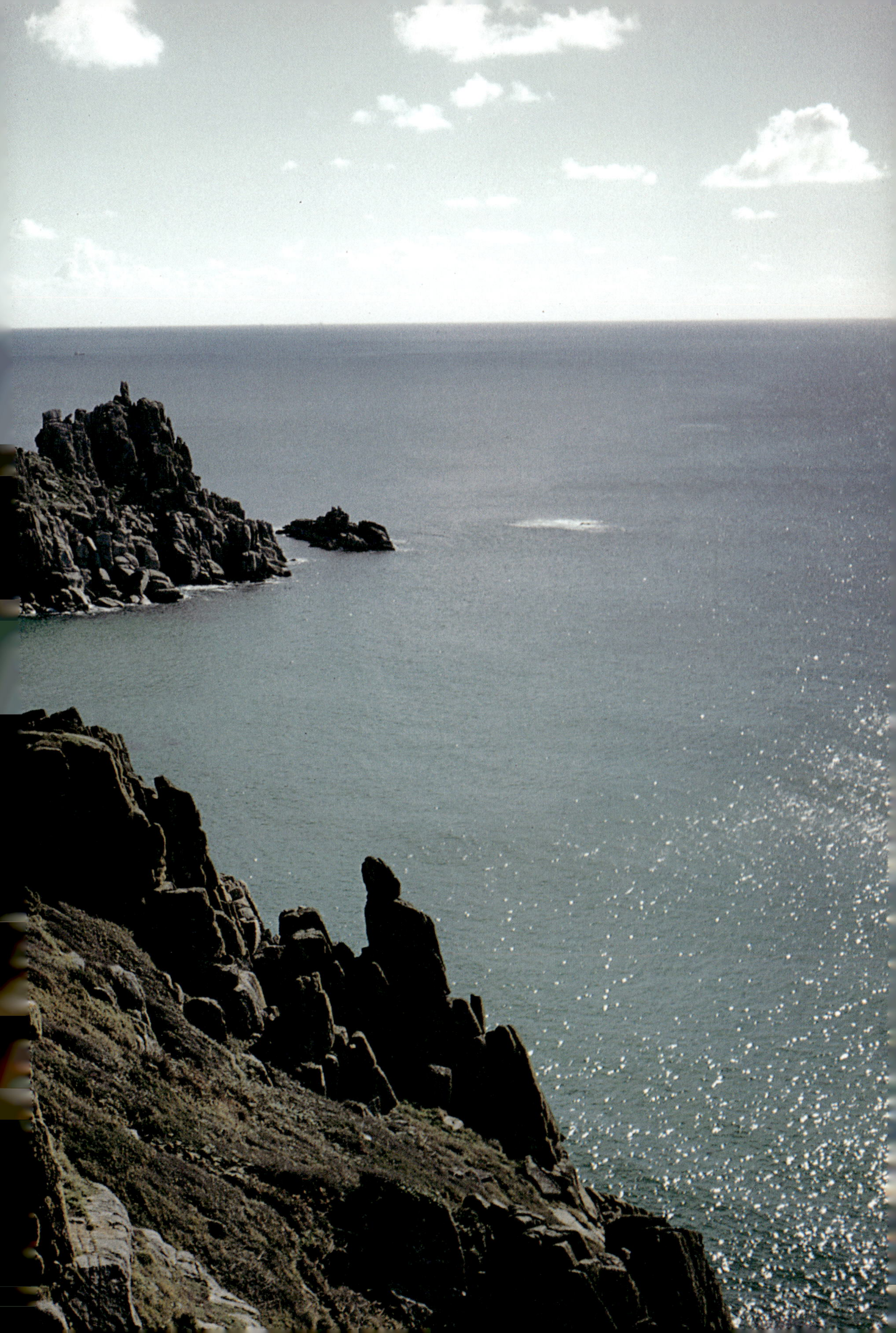

The Logan Rock in the evening

As night approaches, failing light creates a
magical scene of dark rock and silver water.

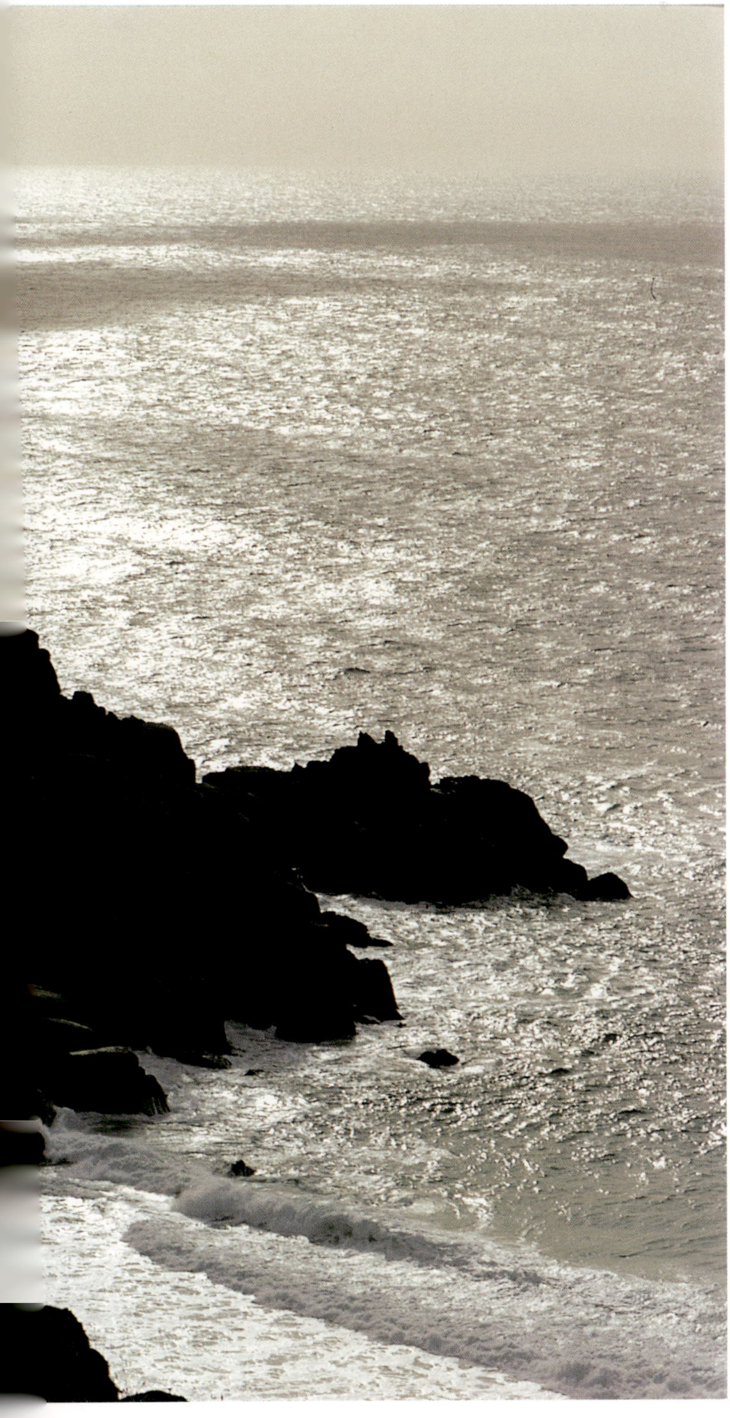

Land's End

The Atlantic surges against the rocks which form the terminal point of some five miles of the most spectacular cliff scenery in England.

Land's End Hotel

(overleaf)

The only satisfying way of making acquaintance with Land's End is to walk the coast path from the Logan Rock round to Sennen Cove, descending when possible to some of the fascinating coves beneath.

The Armed Knight Rock

(overleaf pp 132/133)

Beyond this massive rockpile, the Longships Lighthouse rises 123 ft above the waves.

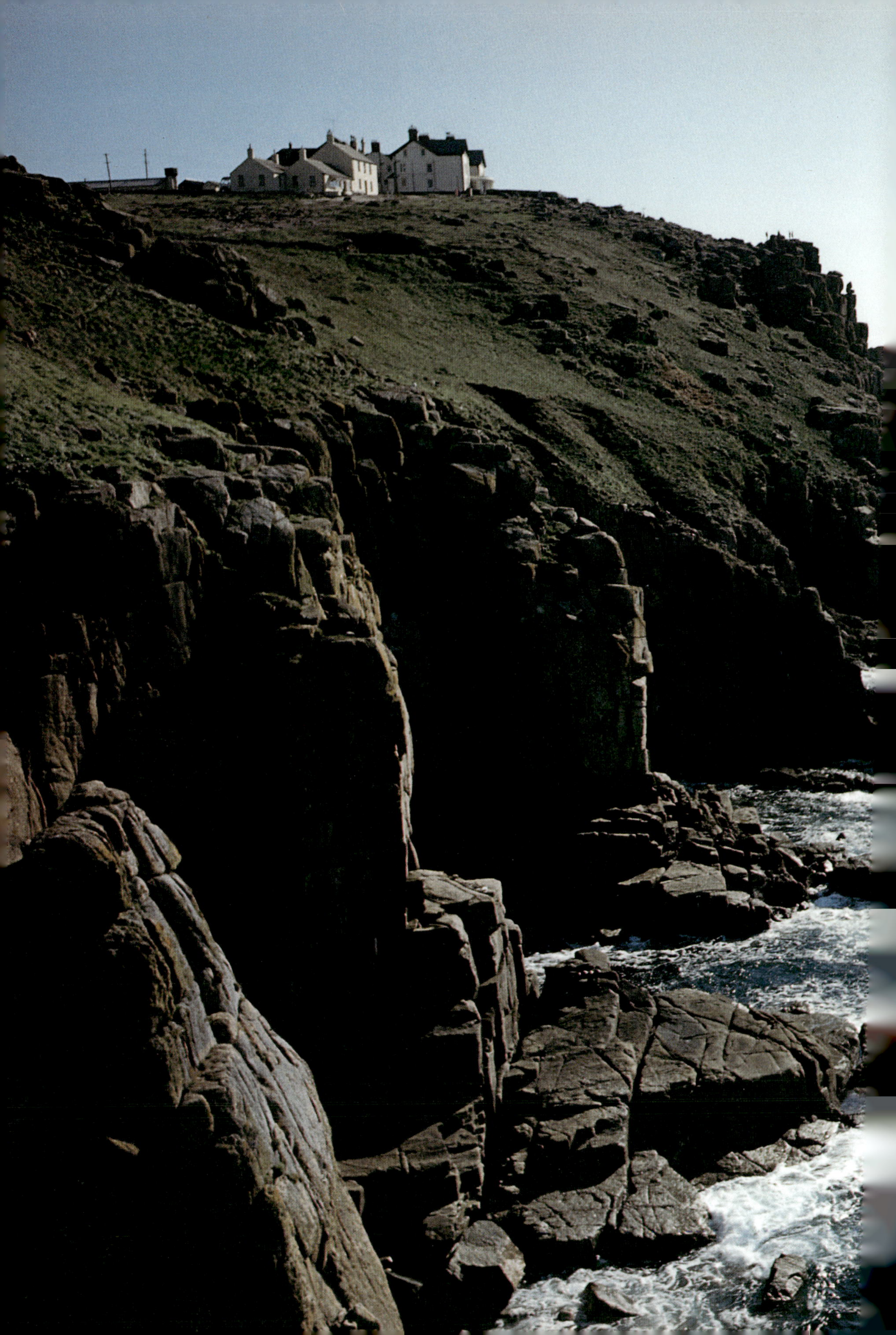

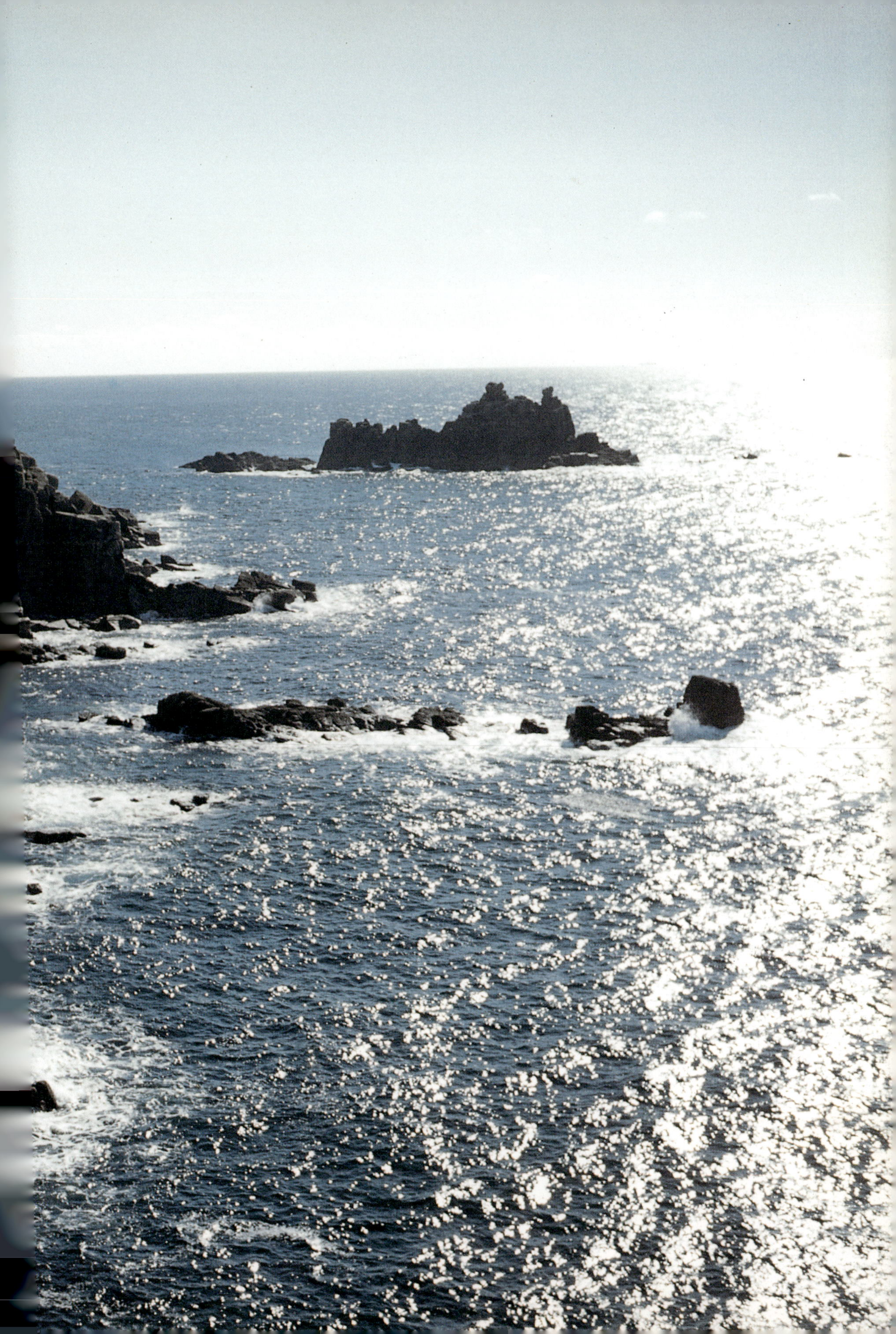

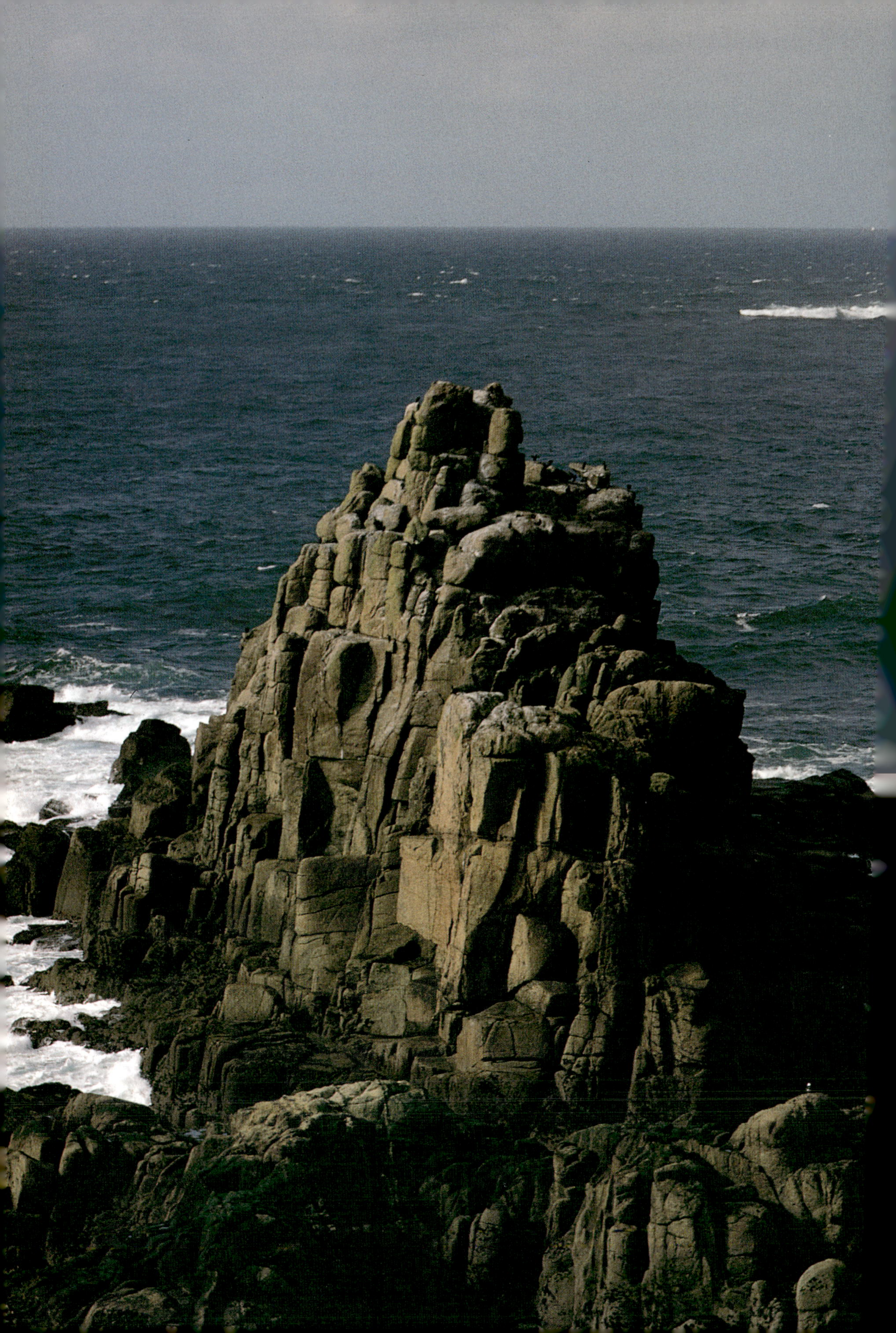

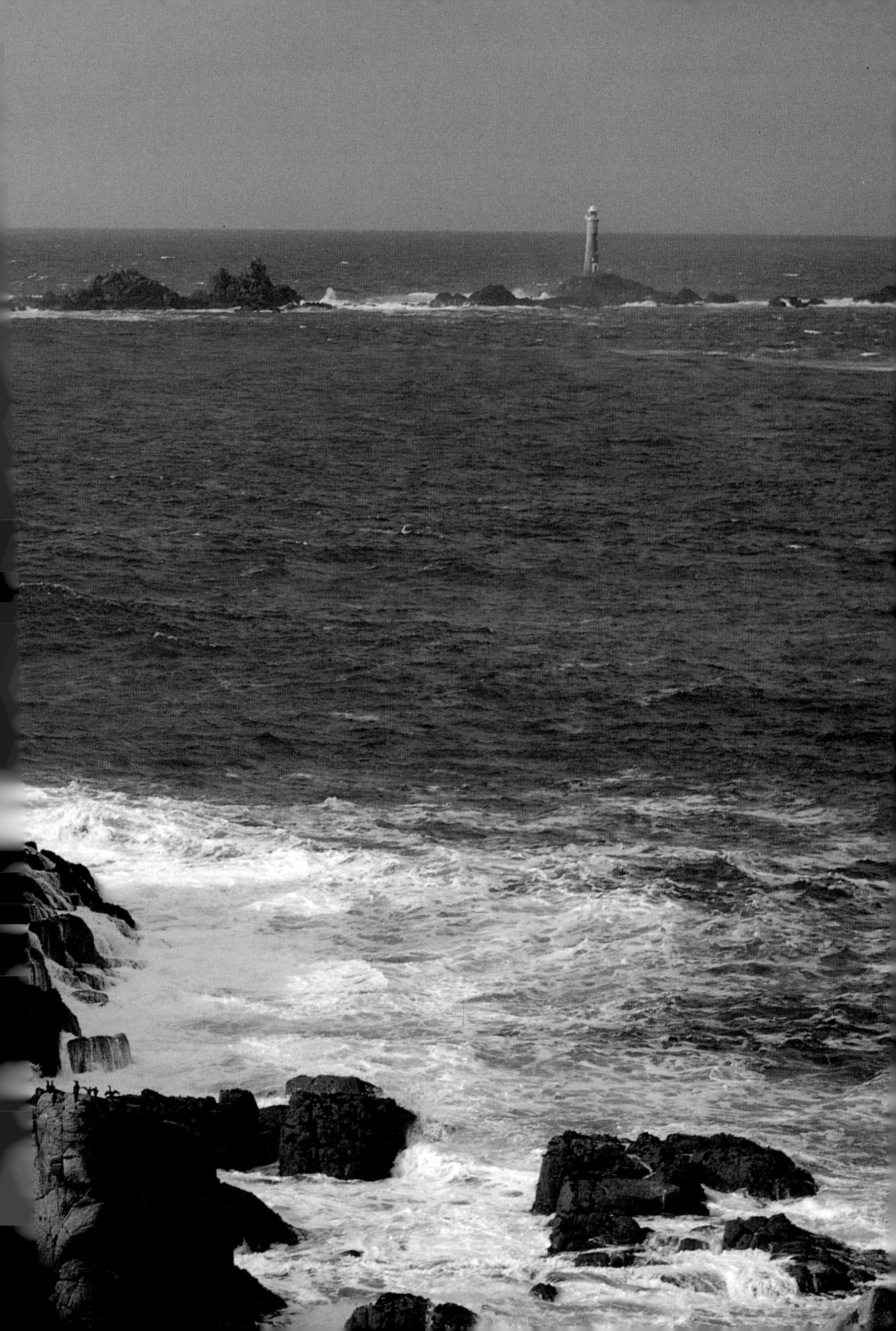

The first and last house in England

The whole of Land's End is a magnet for visitors in summer and for many years they could buy refreshments here. But since the millionaire David Goldstone acquired the tip of Land's End, the house is used as a thriving crafts centre.

Coastguard's lookout
(overleaf)

Not more than a quarter of a mile from Land's End, this coastguard's post stands sentinel over the rocks and waters of this beautiful but dangerous coast. Just out of sight round the headland is Sennen Cove.

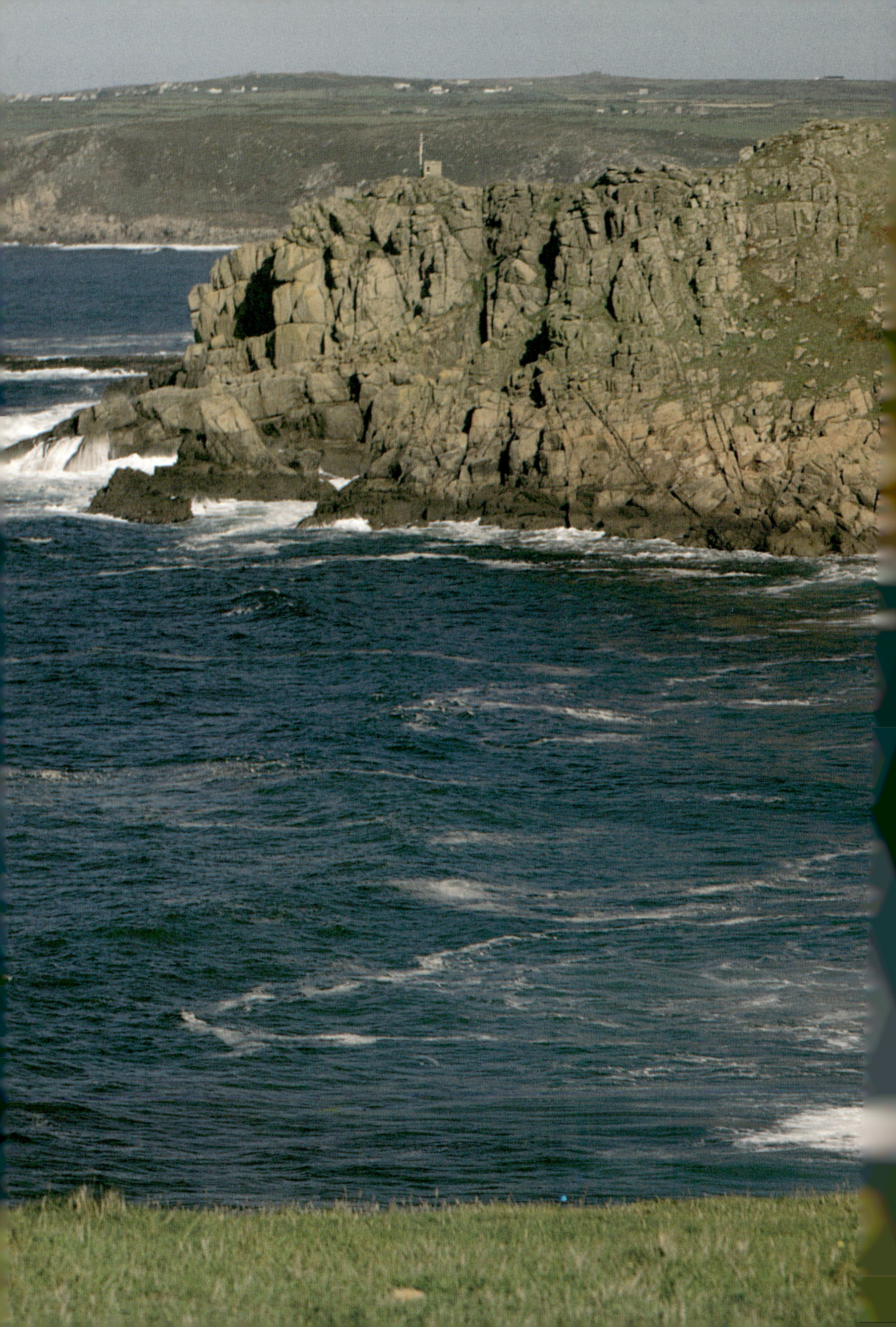

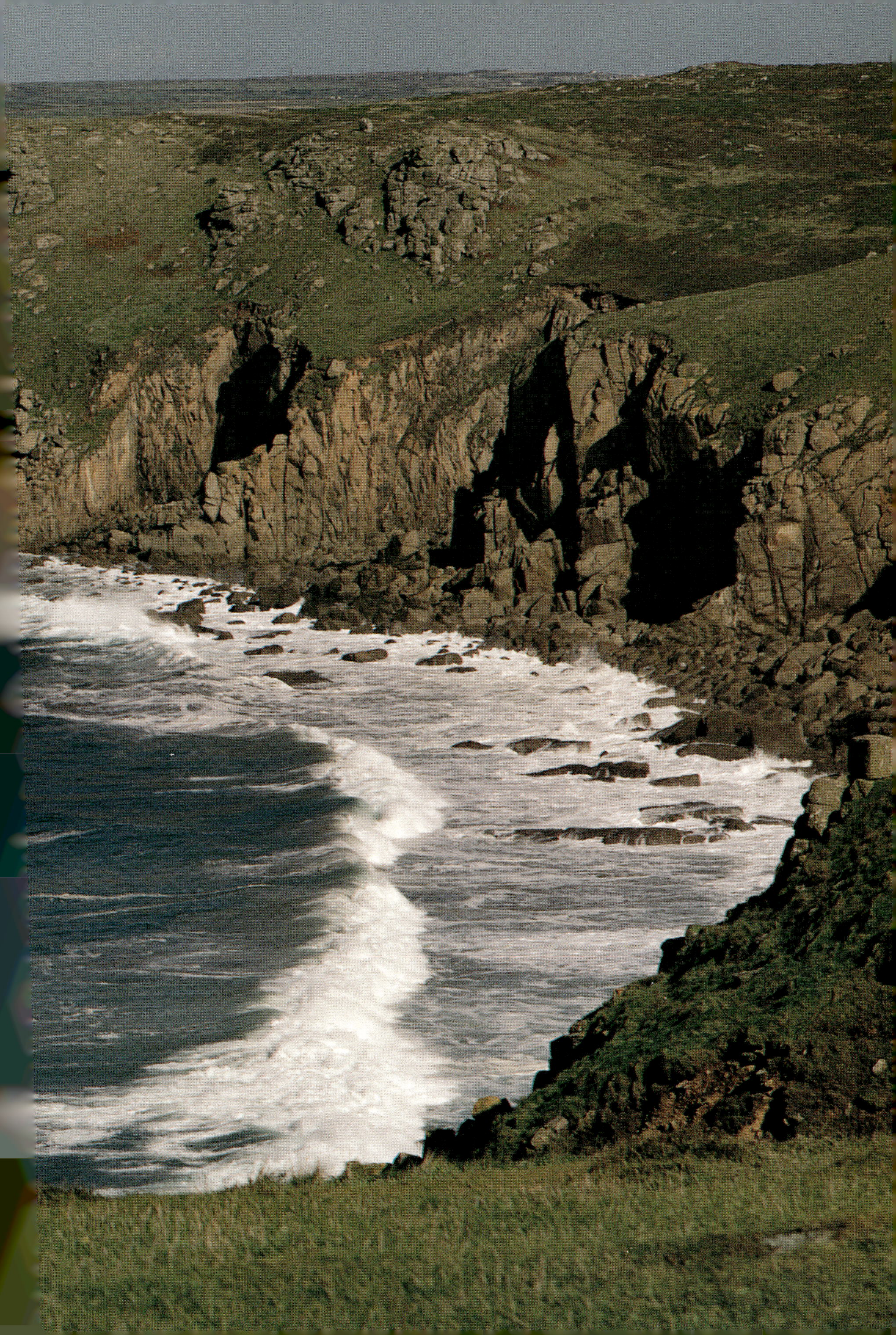

Fishermen at St Ives

This little town, some 20 miles from Land's End, is one of Cornwall's most beautiful holiday resorts. Here fishermen are seen sorting their nets while the tide is out.

The bay of St Ives
(overleaf)

Artists have gravitated to St Ives for many years because of the clear light and freshness of colour to be found there: photographers appreciate it for the same reasons.

The town beach, St Ives
(overleaf pp 142/143)

Though shops and cafés line the quaysides where once were fishermen's cottages, the little port is still one of the gems of the Cornish coast.

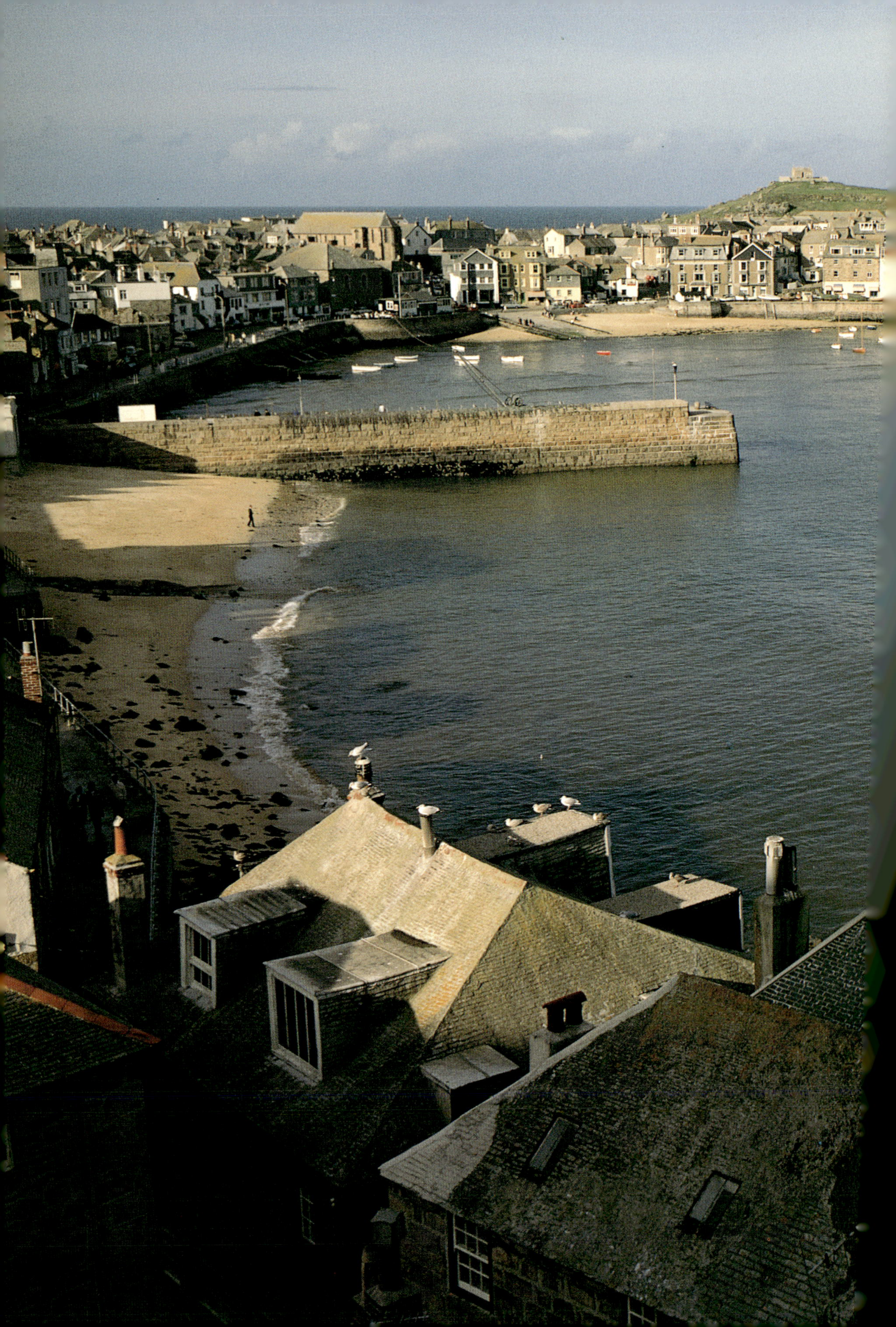

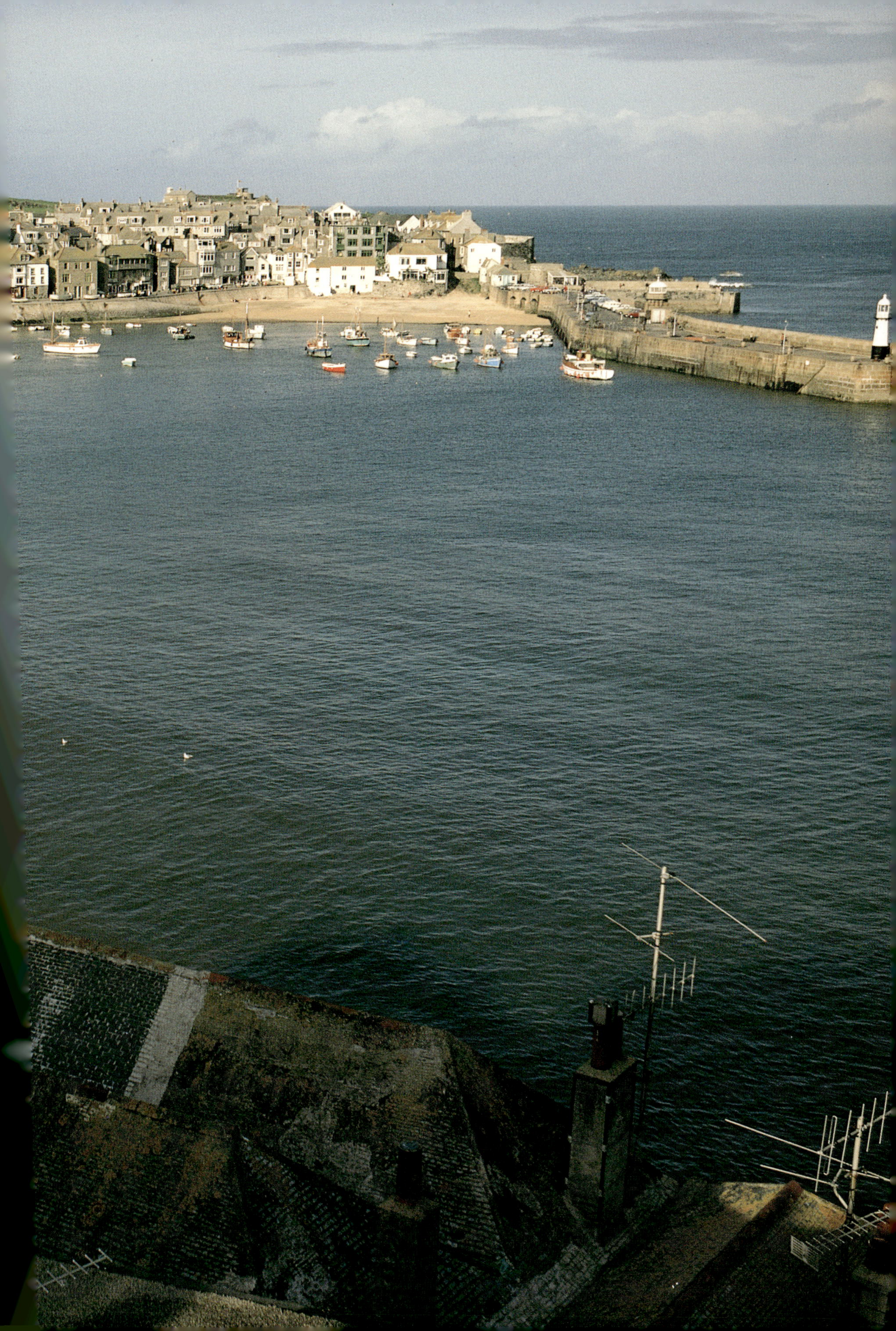

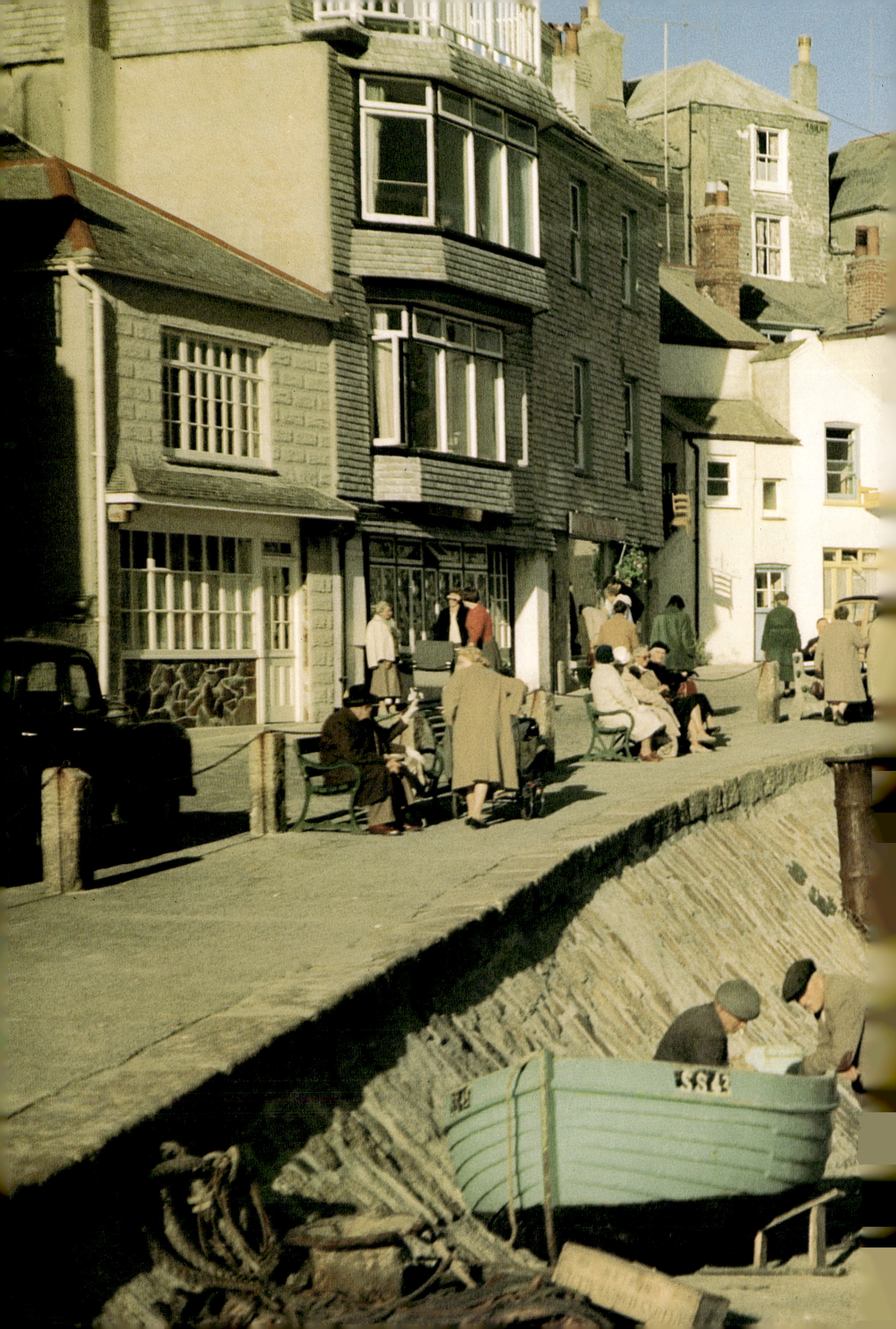

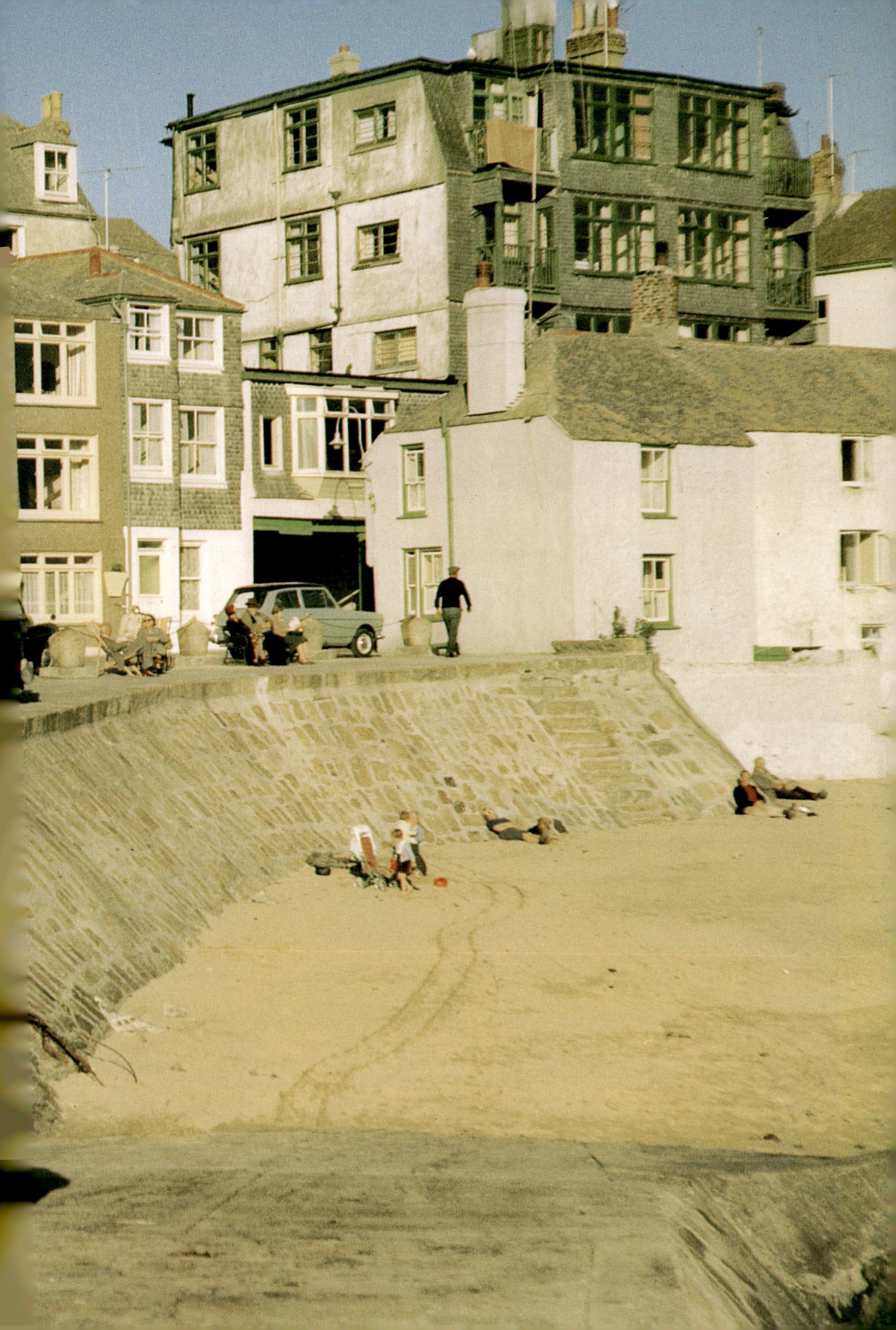

Godrevy lighthouse

This beacon, 4 miles from St Ives and lying just off Godrevy Point, is a dazzling sight in the clear bright sunshine.

145

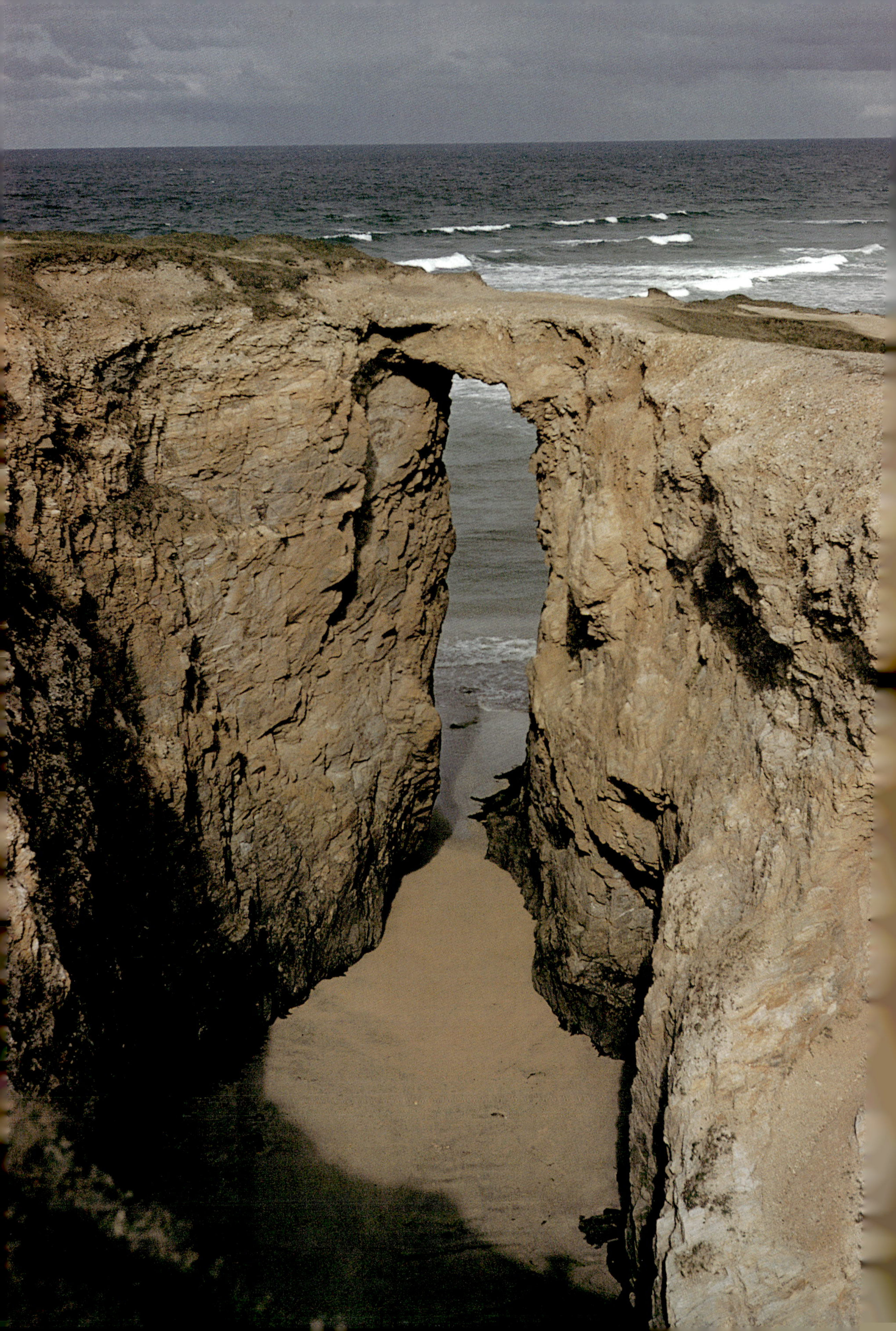

Natural bridge

This amazing inlet, worn by the action of the sea, is to be found in the cliffs near Perranporth.

Hell's Mouth

(here and overleaf)

This spectacular work of Nature looks quite different in rough weather, when huge waves come foaming in among the precipitous rocks. The cave lies between Fishing Cove and Deadman's Cove, and the whole stretch of coastline between Godrevy Point and Portreath now belongs to the National Trust.

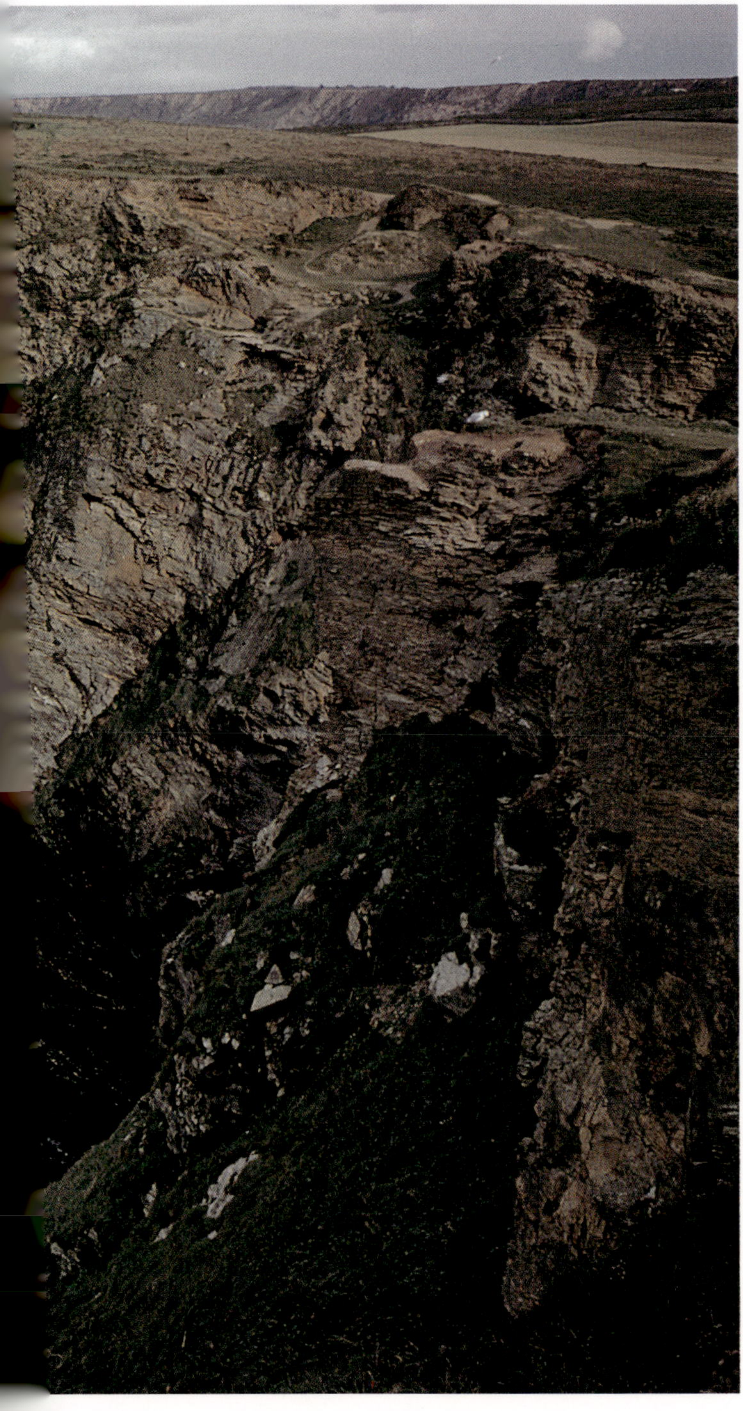

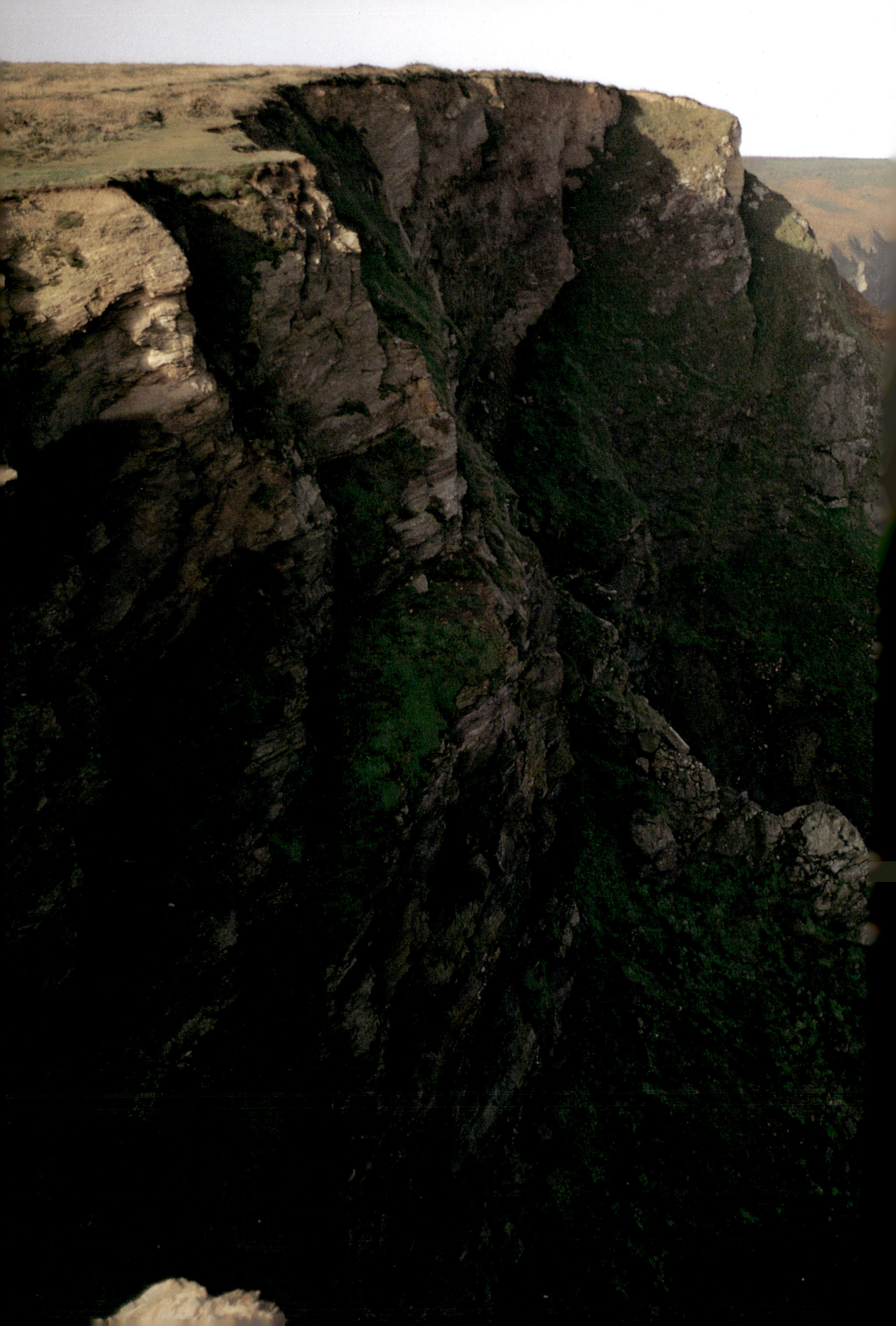

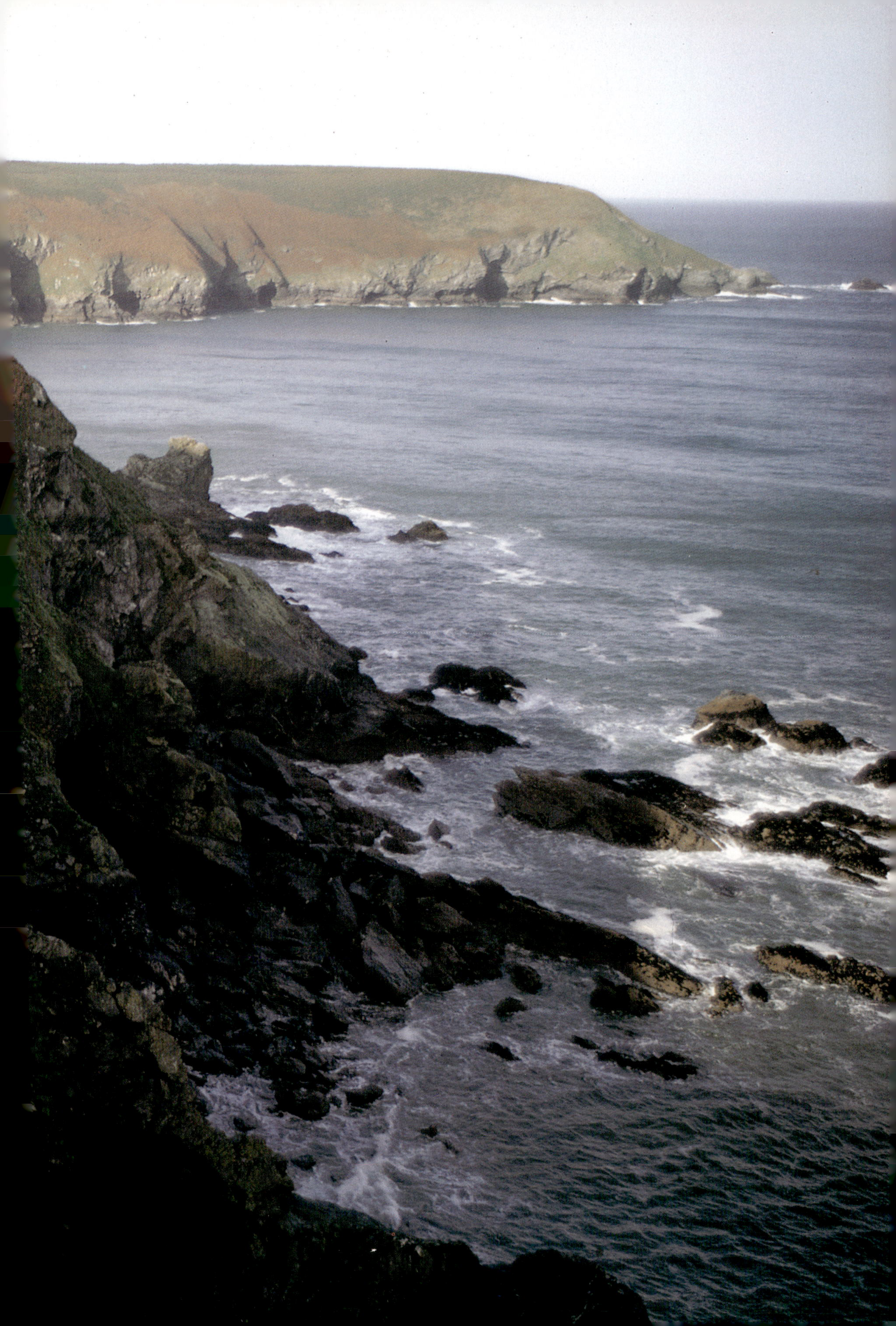

Fistral Bay

This flat and sandy landscape, just to the south of Newquay, is in sharp contrast to the rugged grandeur of most of the North Cornish coast.

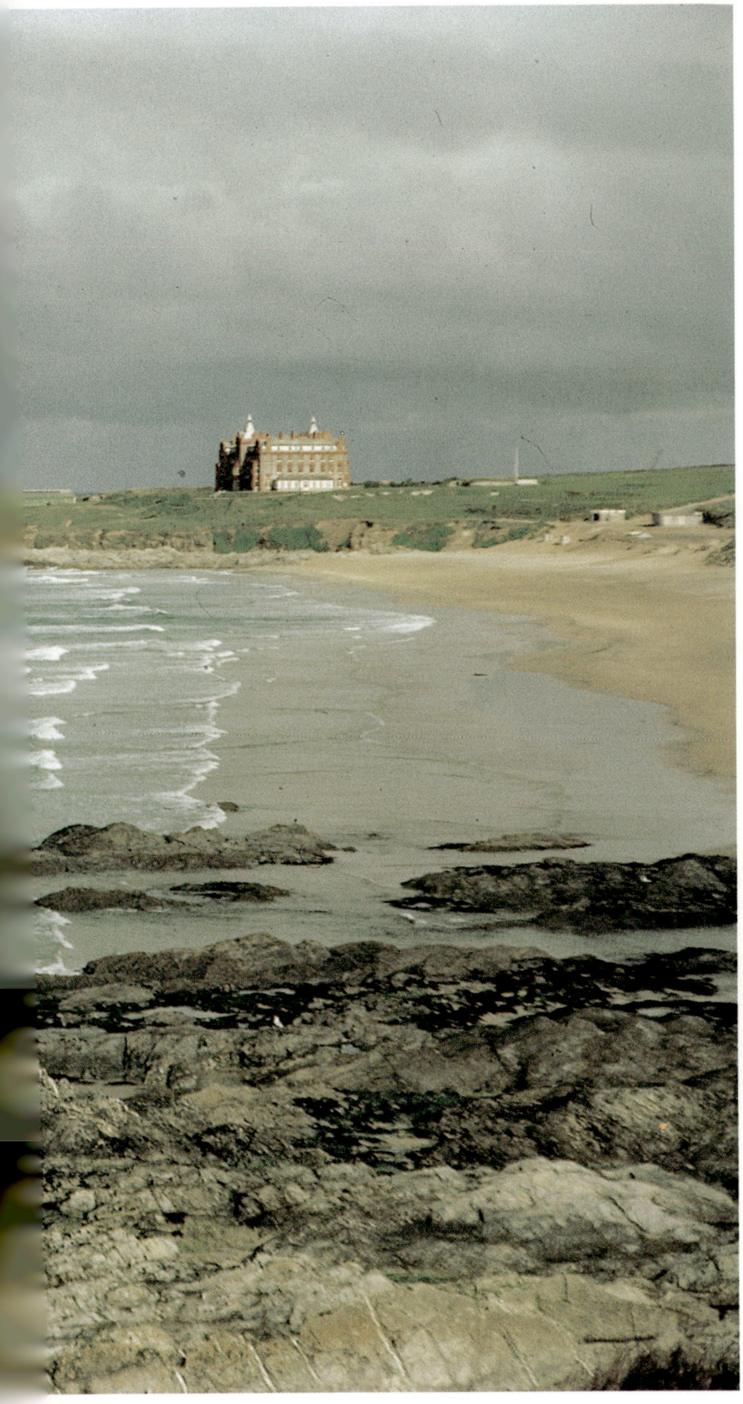

Newquay harbour

Newquay has grown from a small fishing-port into the biggest town in Cornwall, and thousands of tourists flock annually to enjoy its sandy beaches, its rocks and caves.

155

Bedruthan Steps

In the course of all my travels I have not seen an inlet to equal Bedruthan Steps, which I regard as Nature's Cornish masterpiece. It is on the grand scale, with three wild coves ringed by tall cliffs looking down on a collection of weird rock pinnacles that at high tide seem to rise from the sea.

Low tide at Bedruthan Steps
(overleaf)

The best time of day to photograph Bedruthan Steps is at low tide, when the clean sand is attractively patterned and the photographer can work at sea-level without any fear of being cut off. It is also then that one can best appreciate the vastness of the rocky pinnacles, some towering to 100 ft and glistening with white quartz.

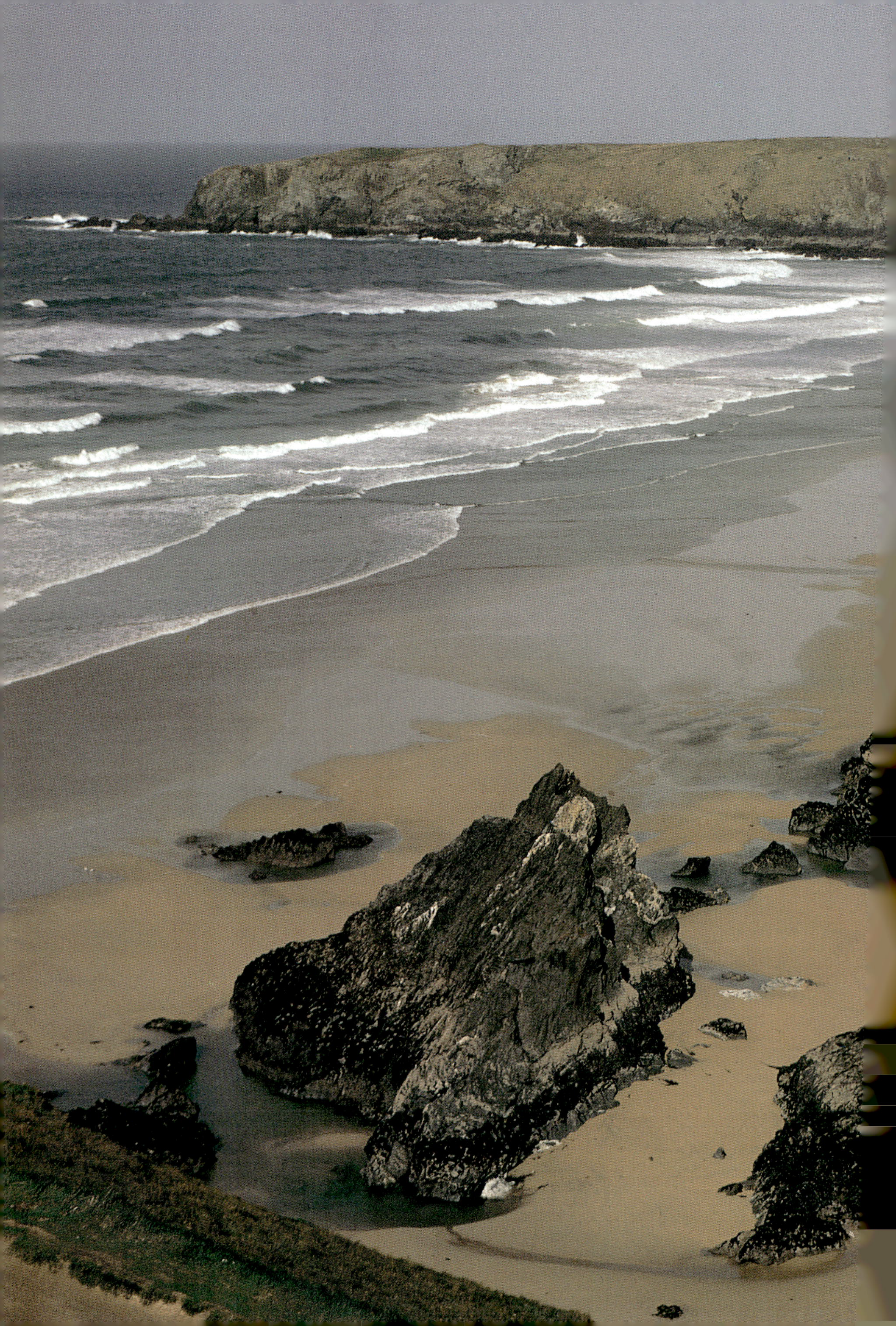

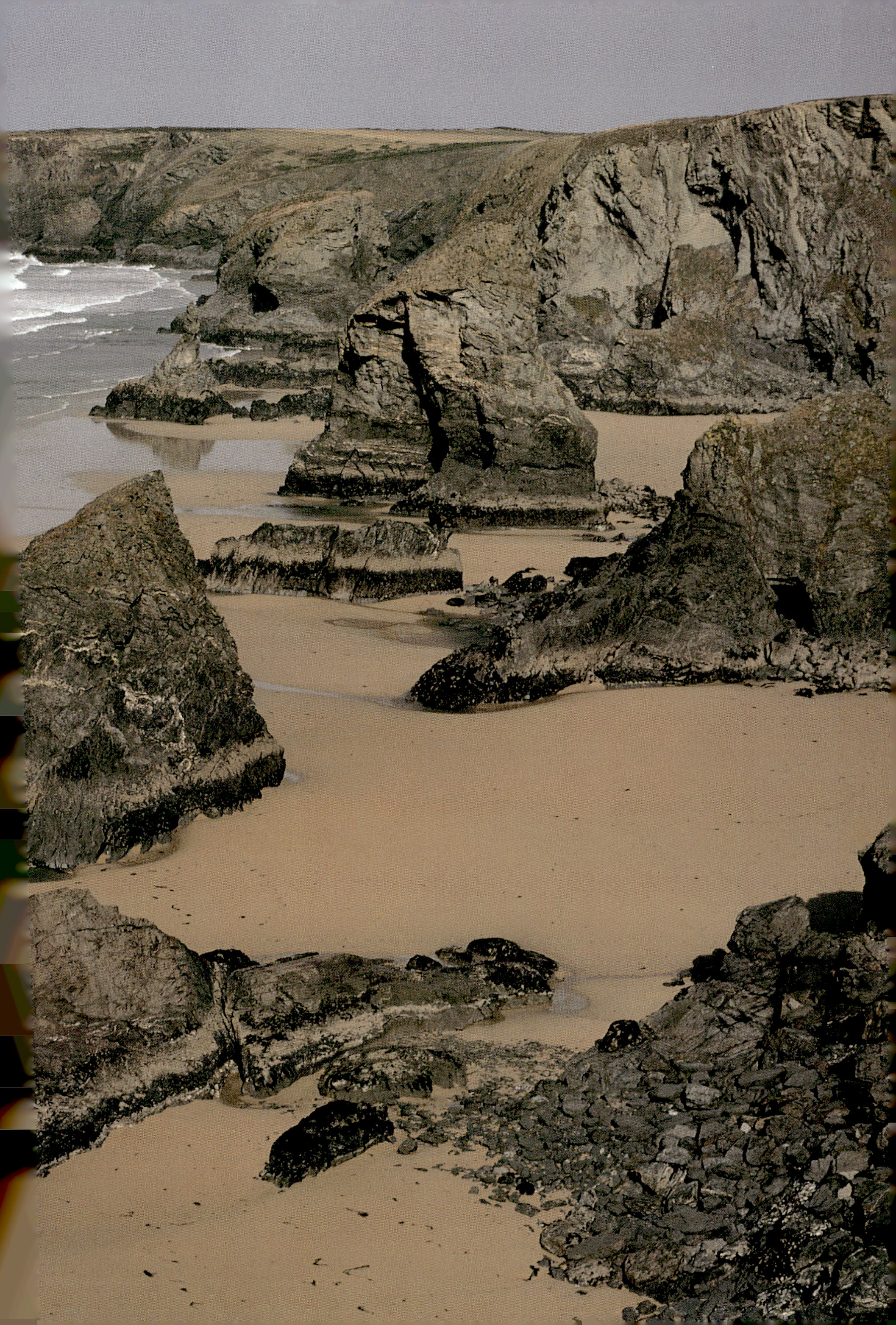

Resting above Bedruthan Steps

The photographer's wife sitting on the thrift-strewn cliffs above this superb inlet.

Padstow harbour
(overleaf)

Both St Patrick and St Petrock are said to have landed here, where the River Camel flows out to sea; and the people of Padstow still celebrate the old fertility dance of the Hobby Horse on May Day.

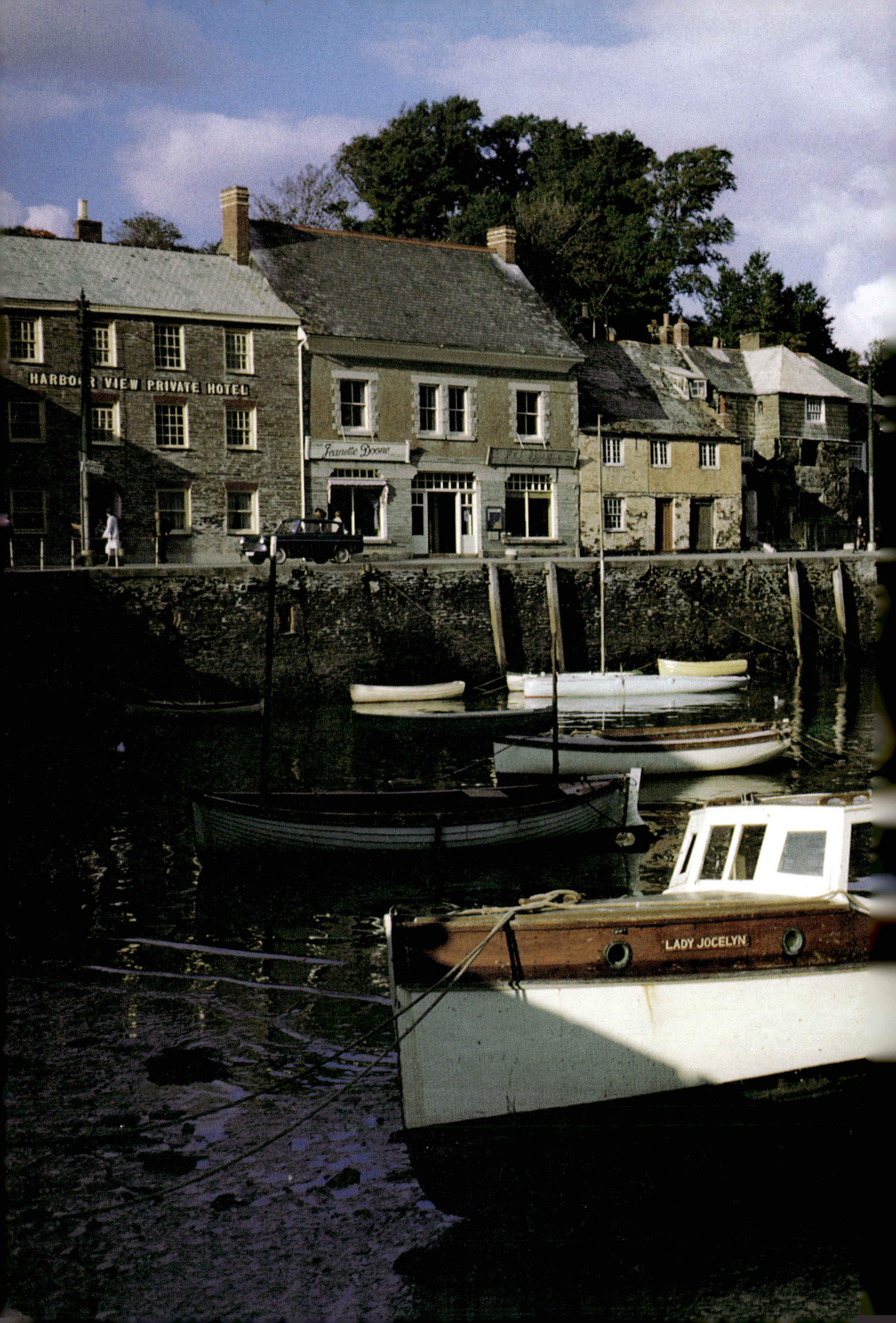
HARBOUR VIEW PRIVATE HOTEL
Jeanette Doone
LADY JOCELYN

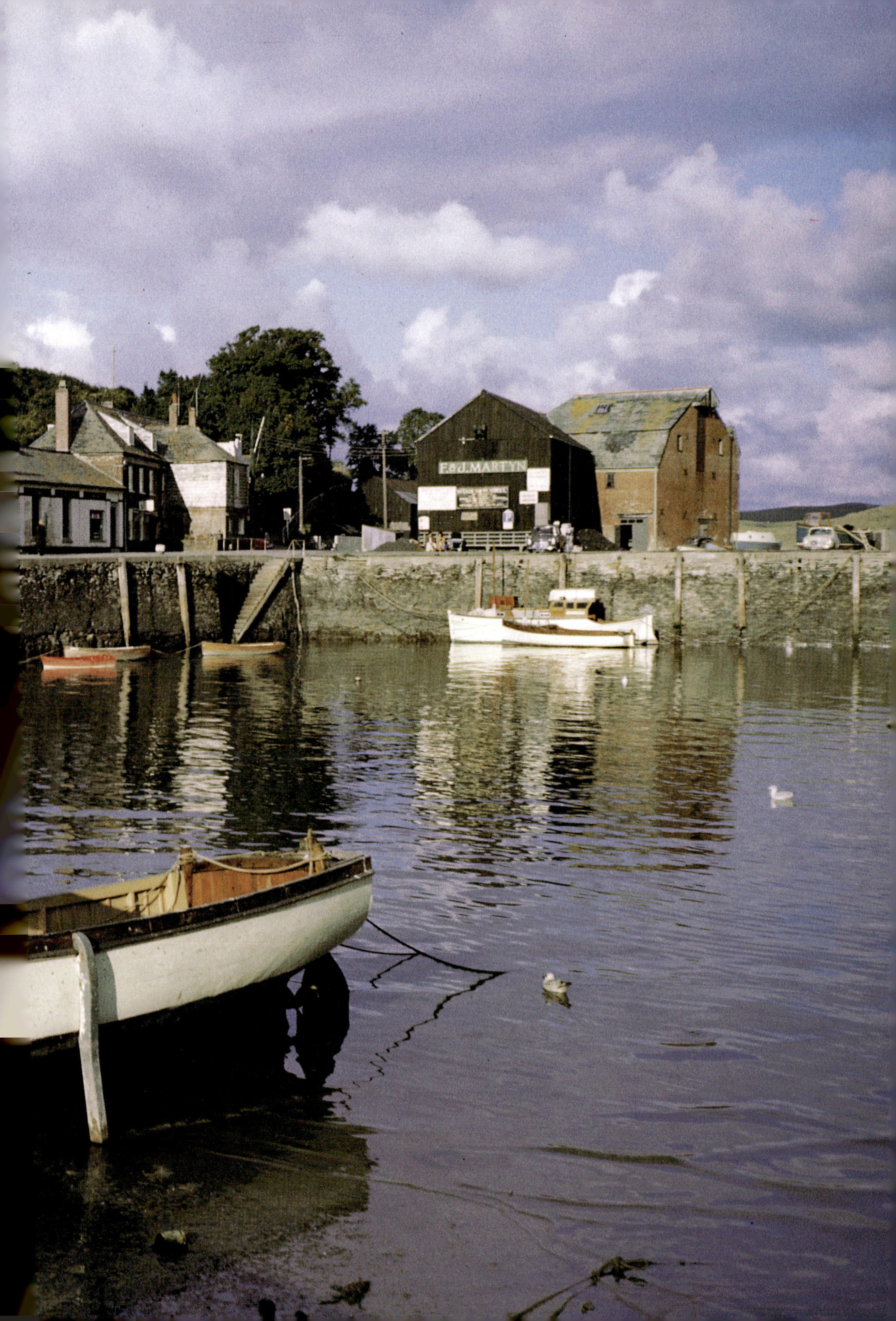
F&J. MARTYN

Wadebridge

Arching 320 ft across the River Camel, this is Cornwall's finest bridge. It was built by Thomas Lovibond in the fifteenth century.

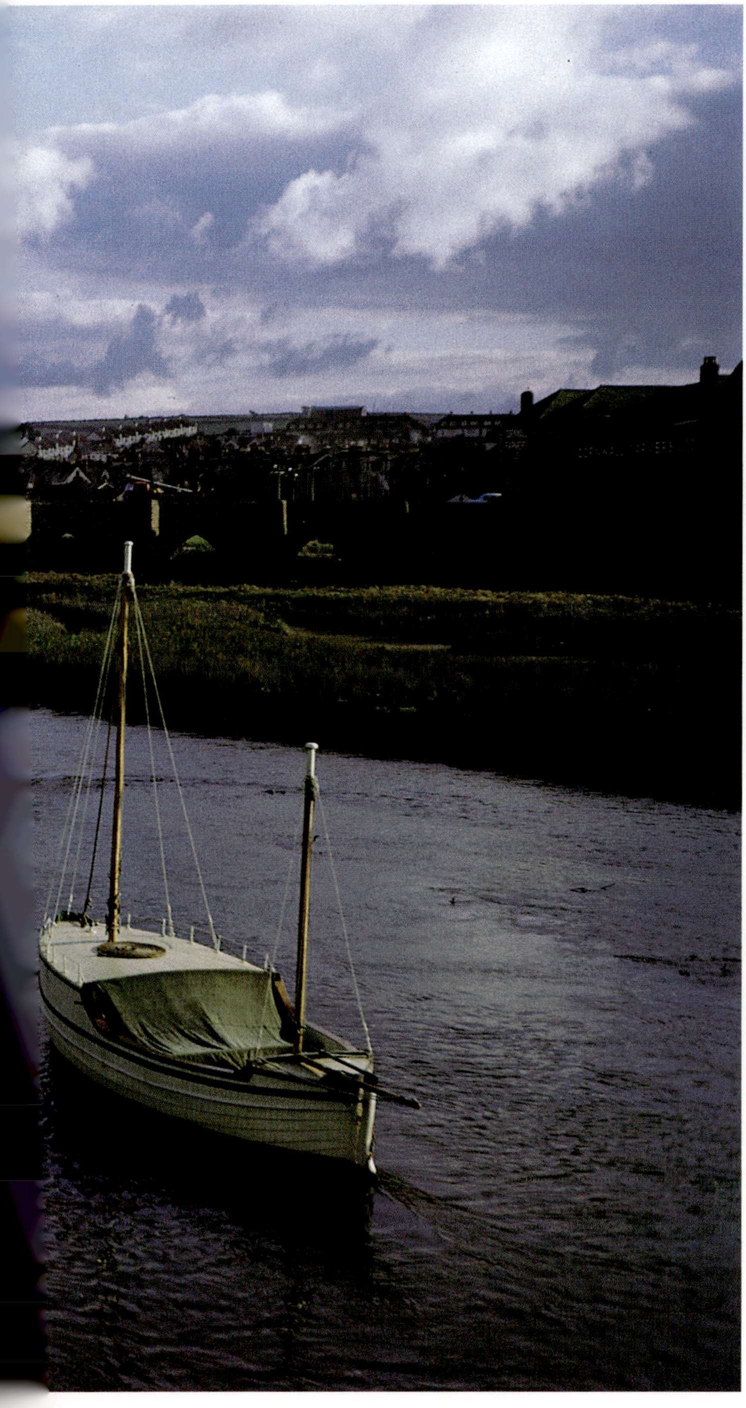

King Domiert's Stone

This was set up on the road from Dobwalls to St Cleer, to commemorate a ninth-century Cornish king who was drowned.

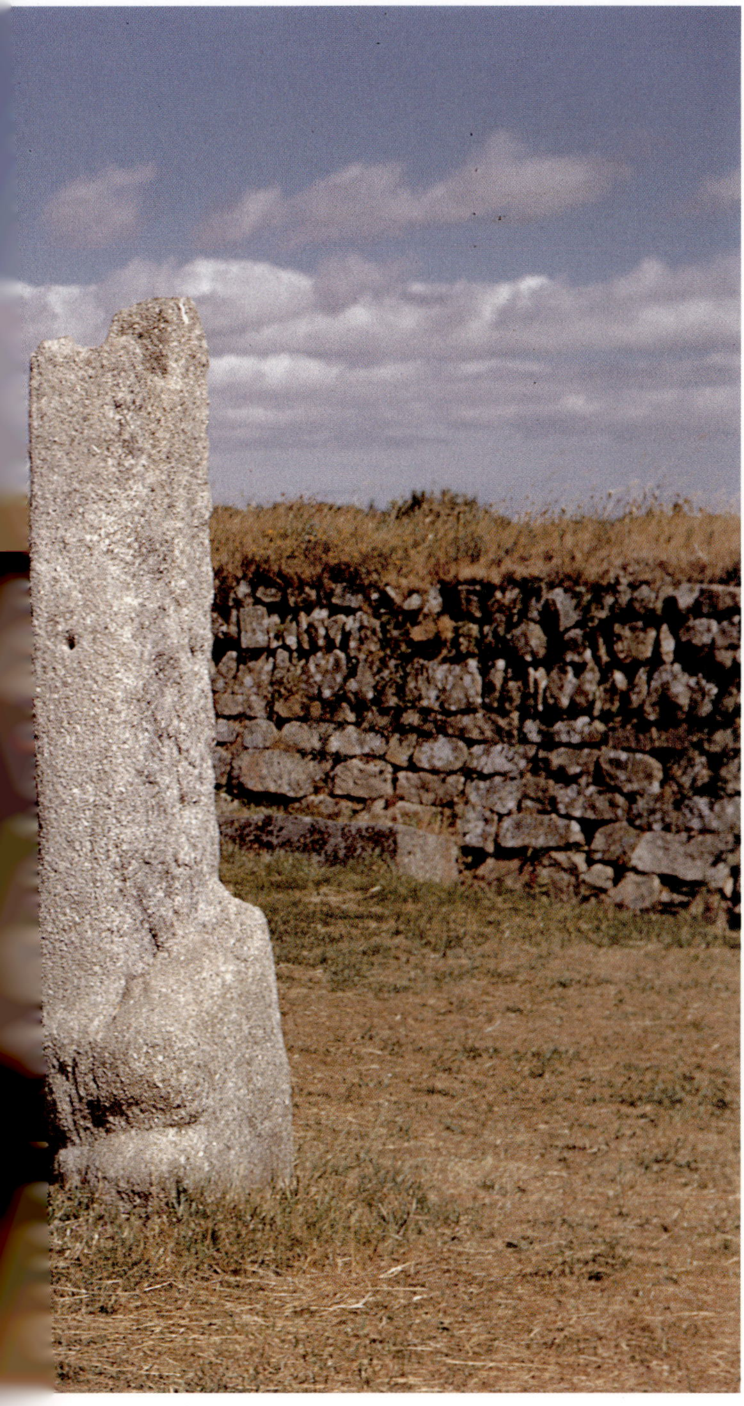

Trevethy Quoit

This astounding and well-preserved cromlech has a giant capstone measuring 14 ft by 9 ft. It stands in the corner of a field, set back from the road that runs from St Cleer to Darite.

The Hurlers

(overleaf)

Follow the road on from Darite to Minions, and you will see on your left these two circles of standing stones, part of the West Country's rich heritage of prehistoric remains.

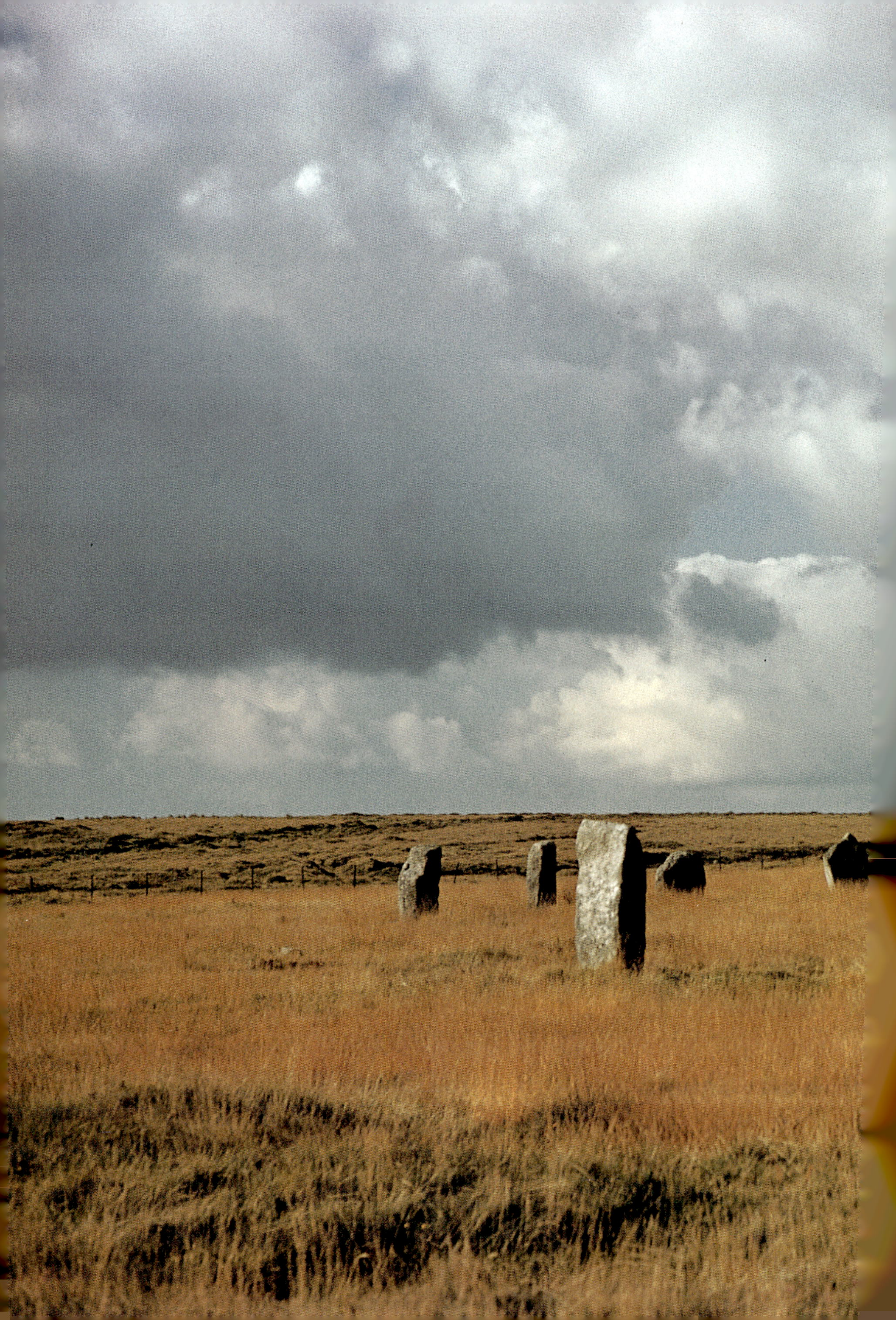

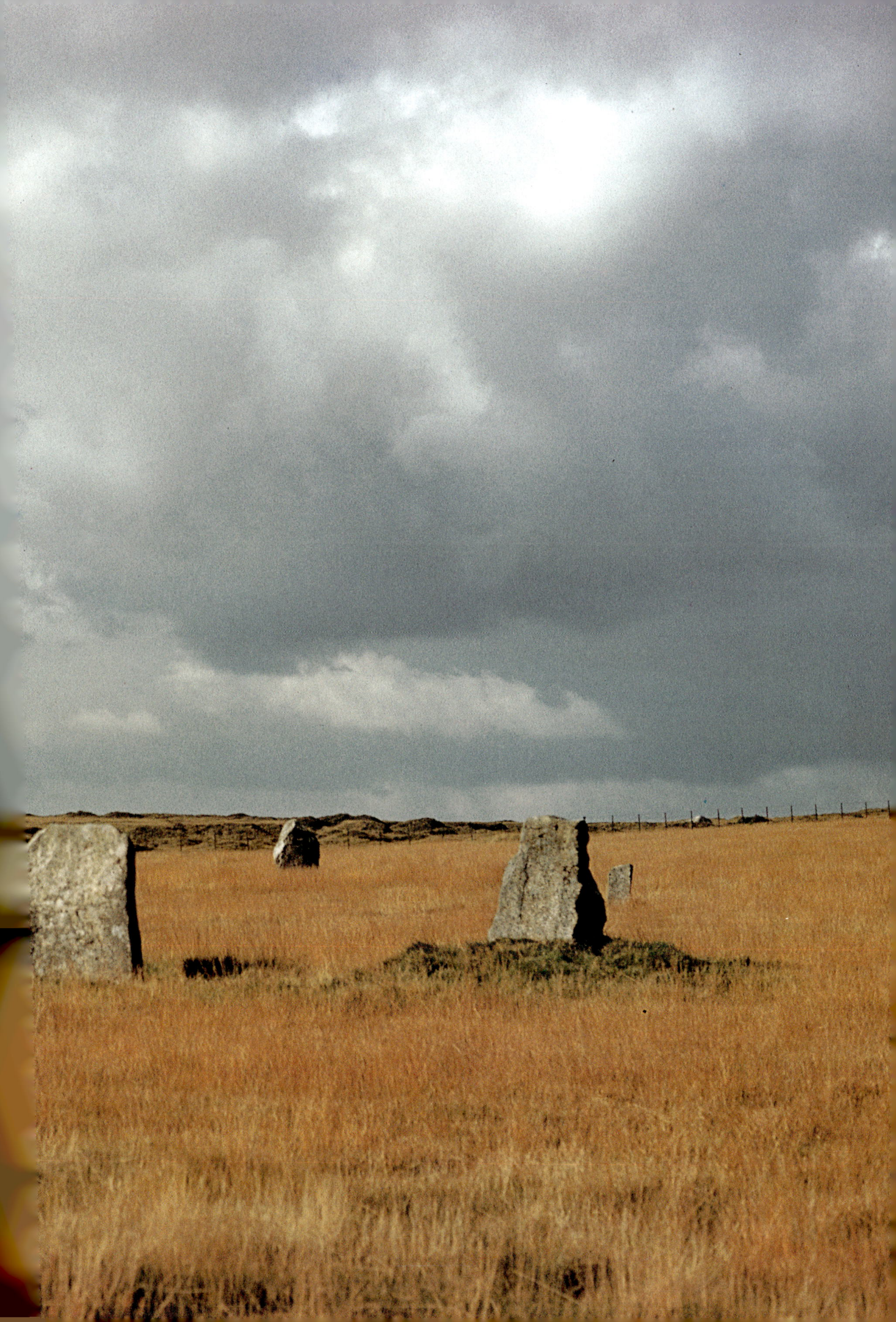

Trevethy Stone

This ancient Celtic cross is not far from the Hurlers: when photographing such isolated stones, cloudscapes are an essential ingredient of the picture.

173

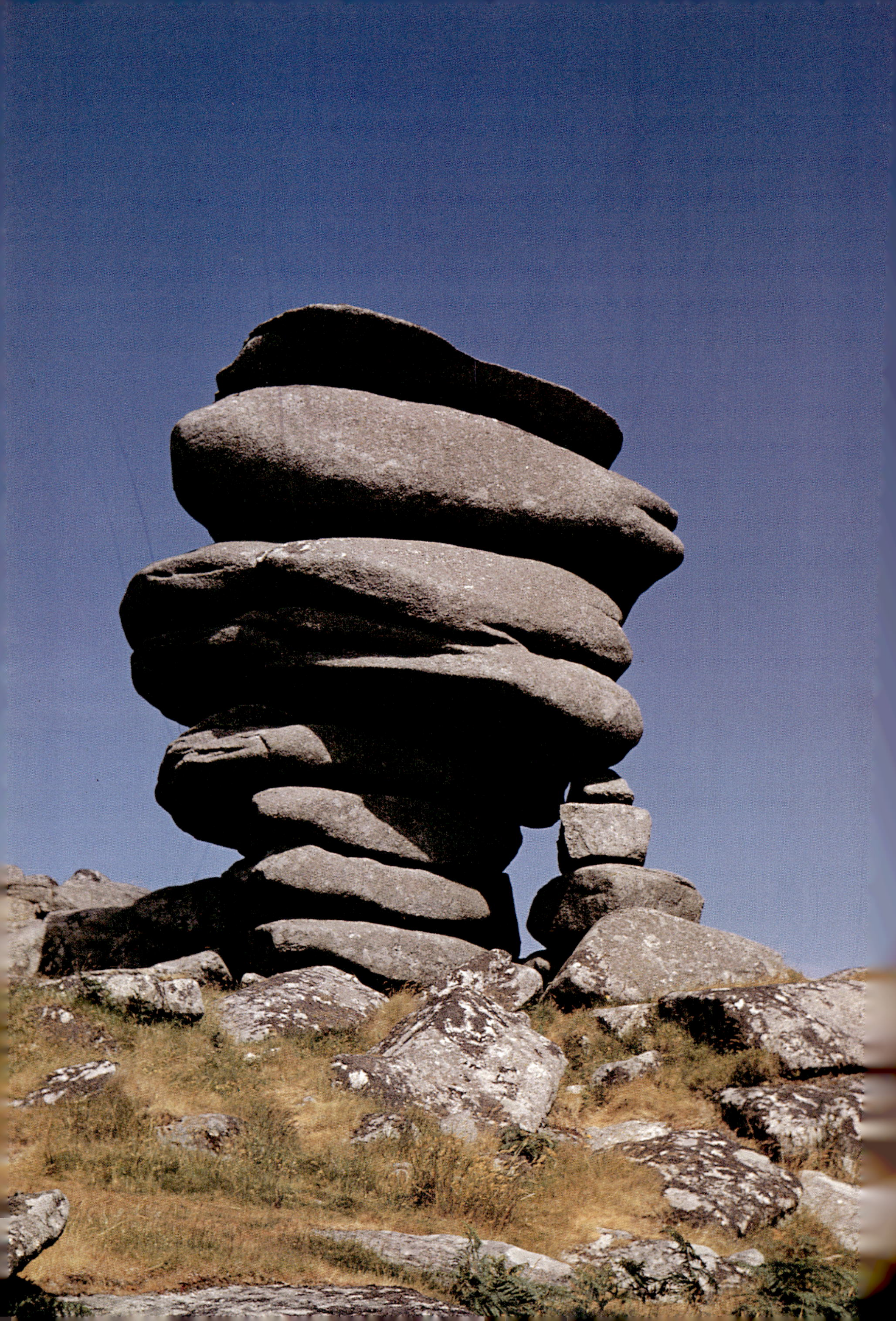

The Cheesewring

This wonderful collection of precariously balanced granite rocks is to be found just through the village of Minions, on the road to Henwood. The top stone is some 34 ft in circumference, and the whole pile towers to a height of 29 ft.

Bodmin Moor

(overleaf)

The road across this bleak and comparatively featureless expanse of moorland is dominated by Brown Willy and Rough Tor, seen in the background.

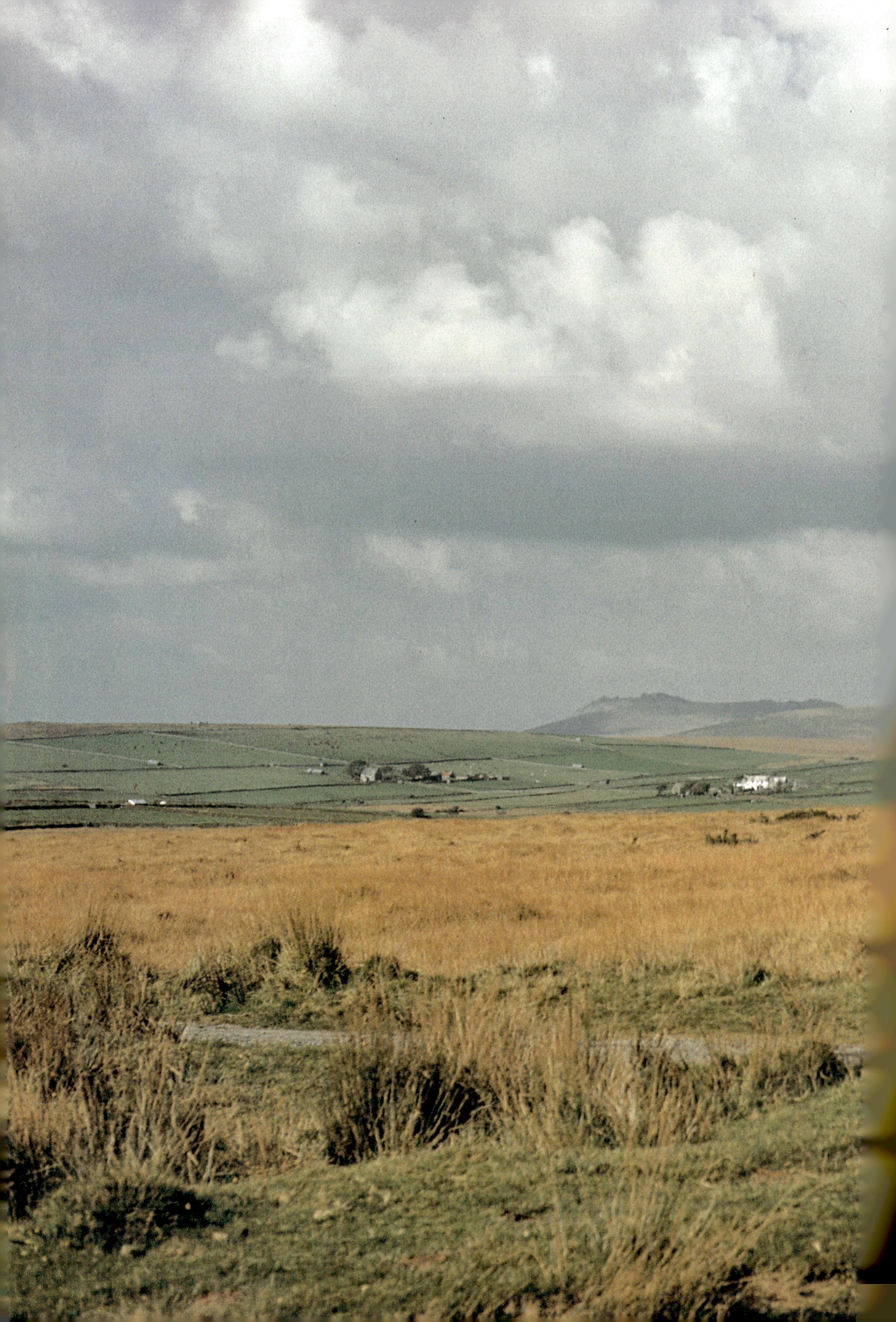

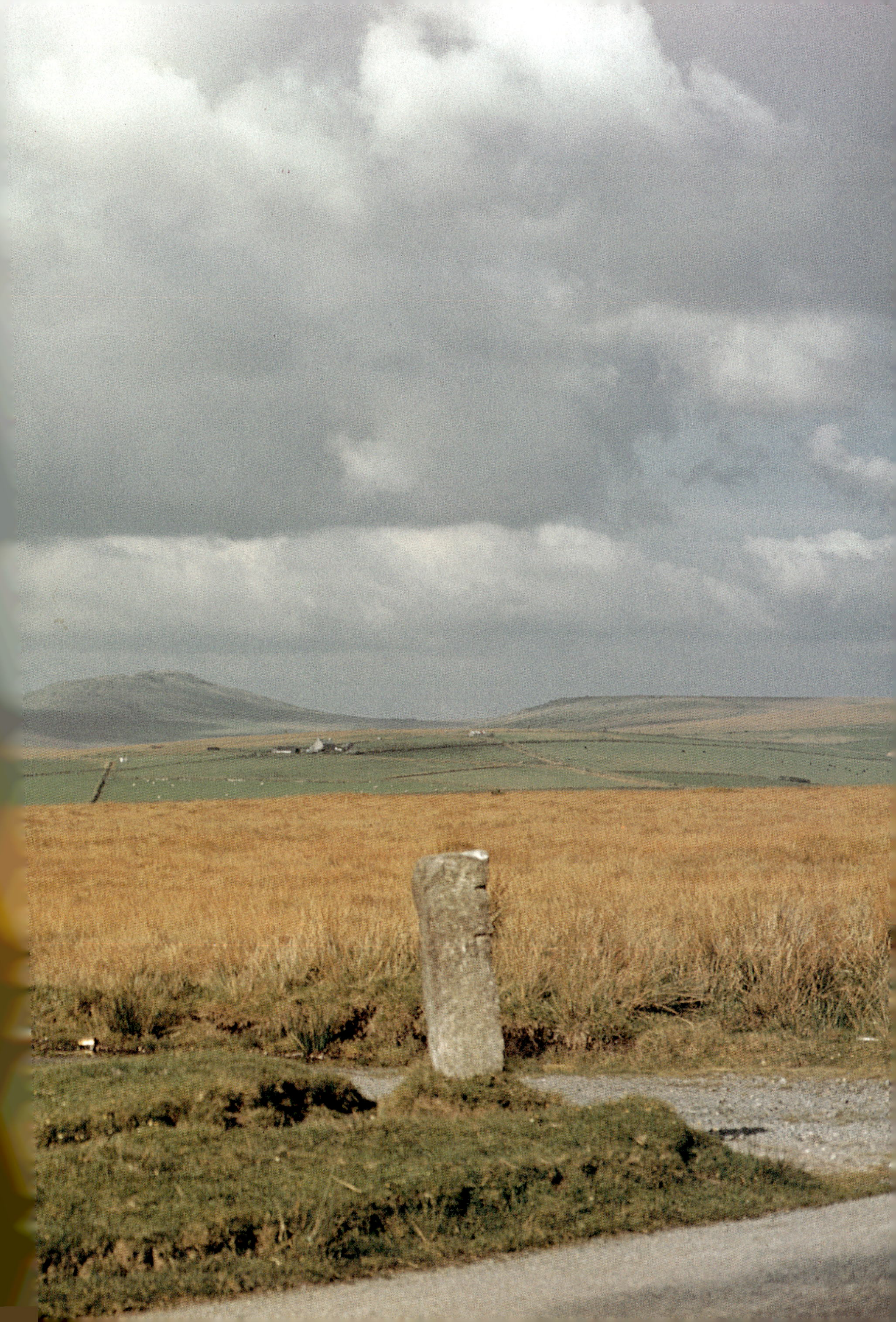

Jamaica Inn, Bolventor

In the heart of Bodmin Moor stands this old granite and slate-clad building, which is said to have once been the haunt of smugglers. It was immortalized in a famous novel by Daphne du Maurier.

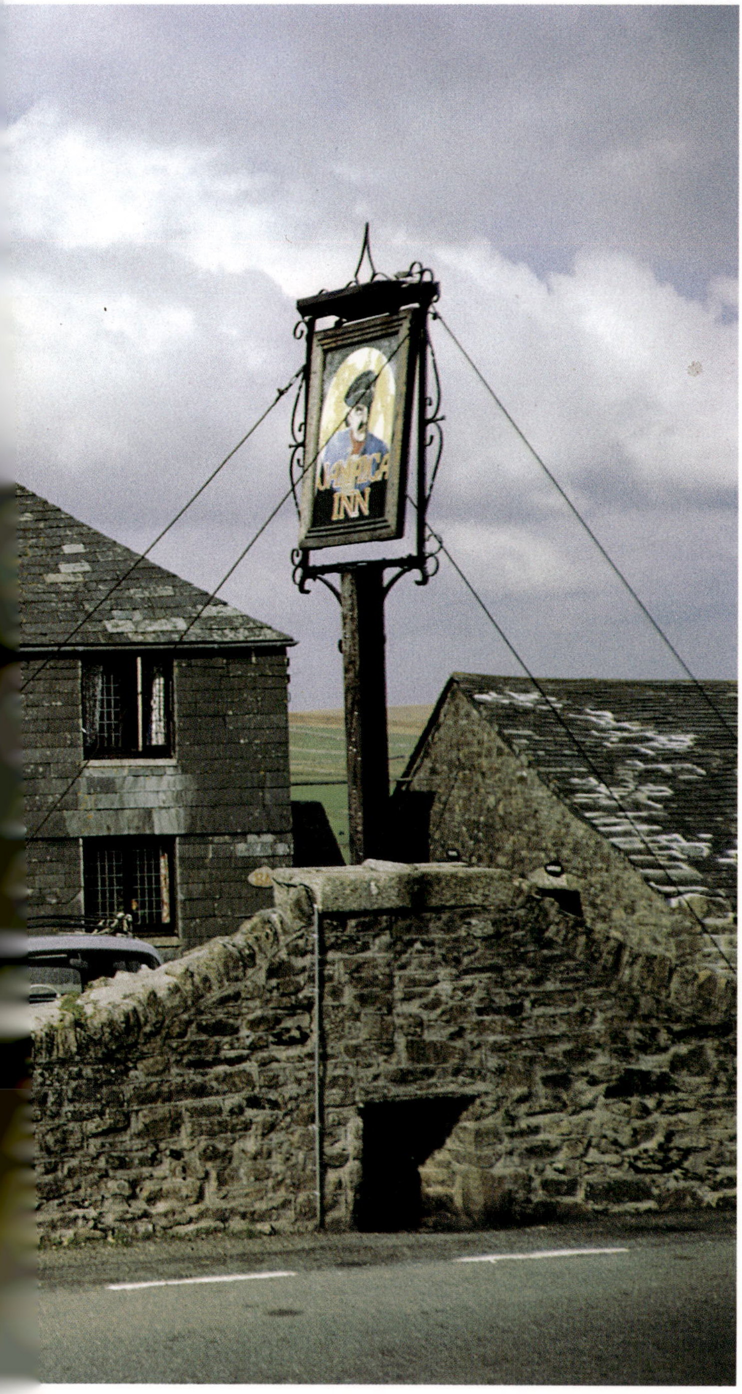
INN

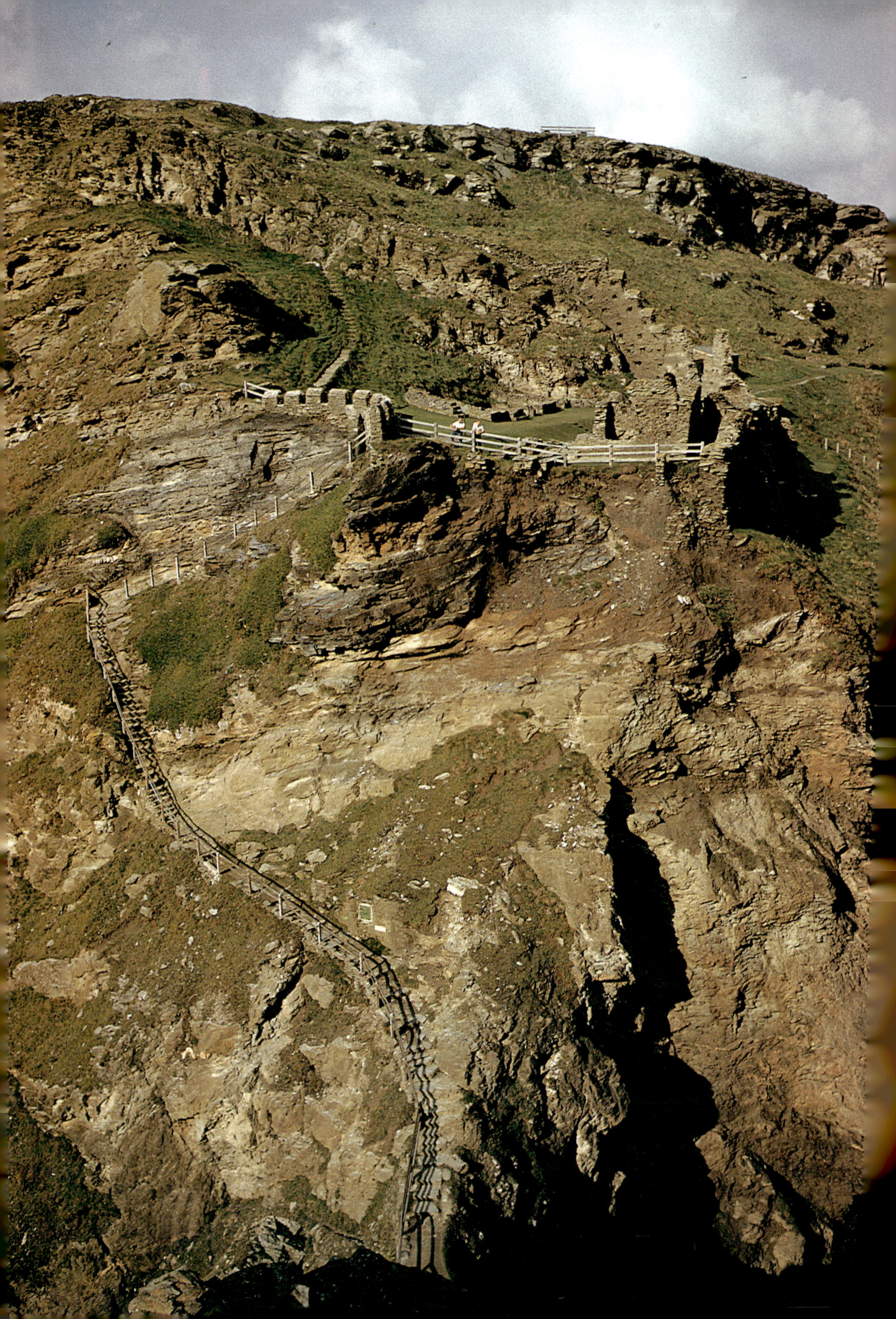

Tintagel

This rocky peninsula, jutting out into the rough sea and surrounded by magnificent cliffs, is approached down a steep, rutted track from the village, and across a precarious wooden bridge.

King Arthur's castle

(overleaf)

Though visitors are drawn to these ruins by the romance of the Arthurian legend, it is in fact more likely that this was the site of one of Britain's first Celtic monasteries, dating back to the fifth century.

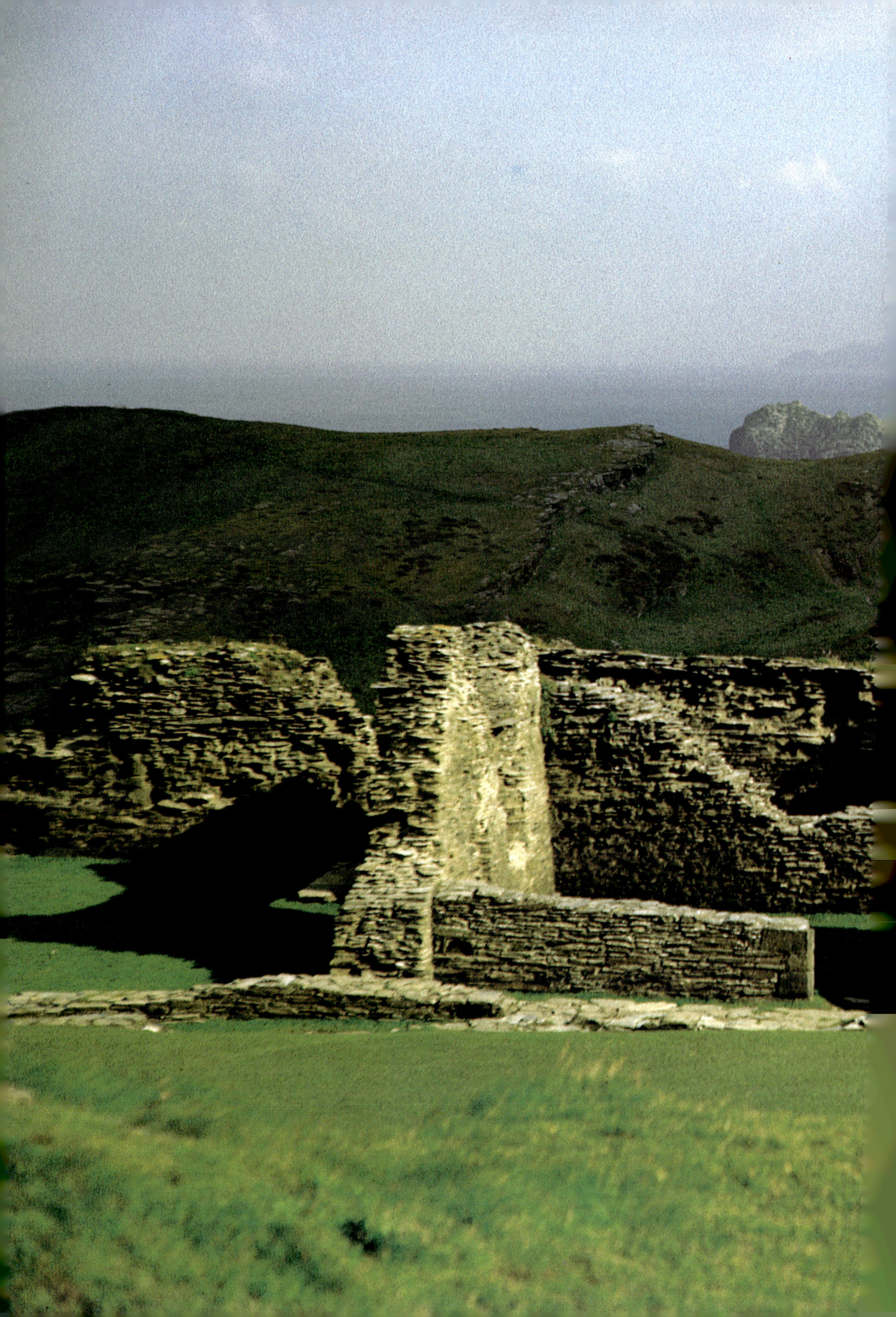

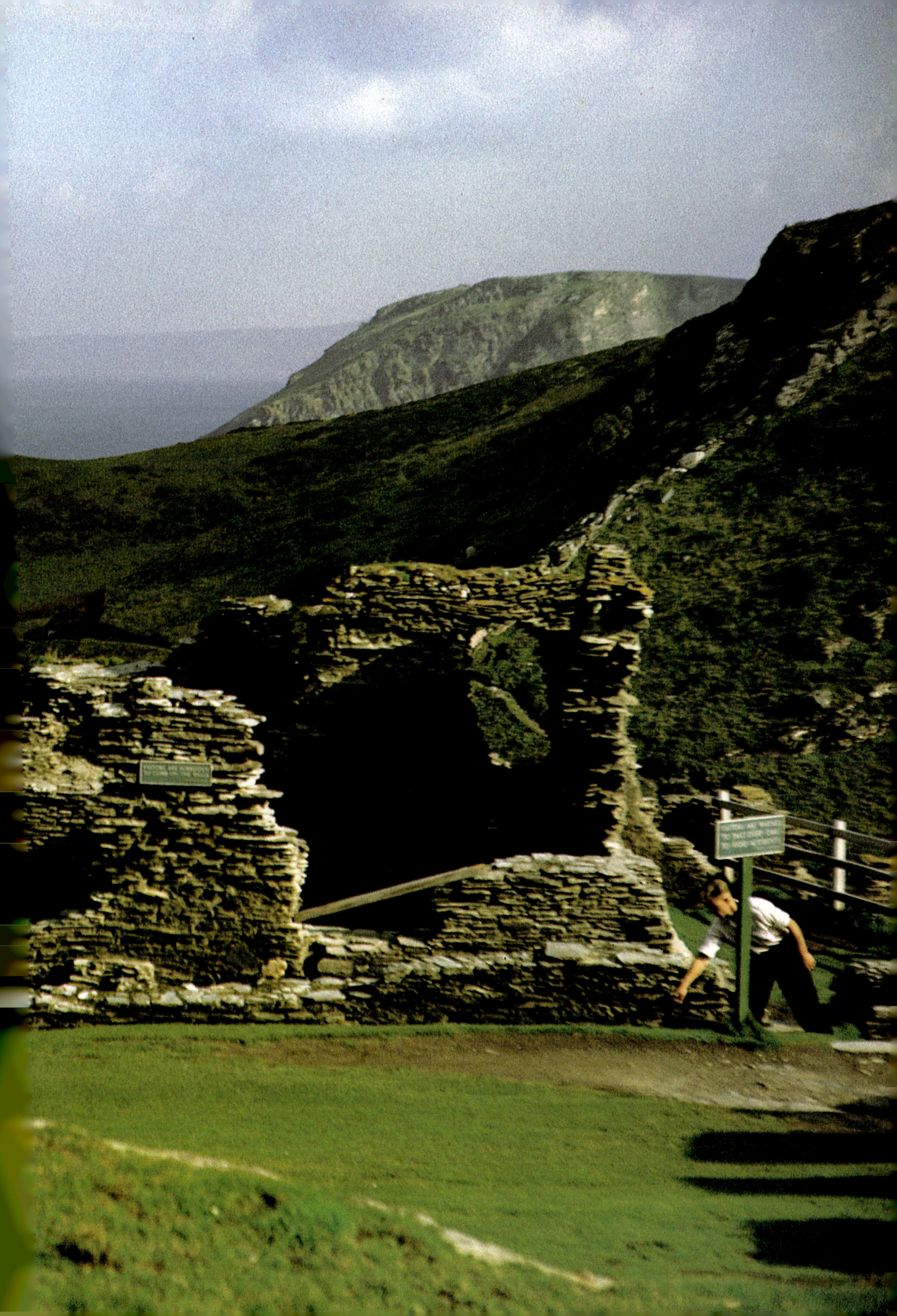

Boscastle

This is one of the most beautiful and unusual of all Cornish harbours, and is surrounded by fine cliff walks.

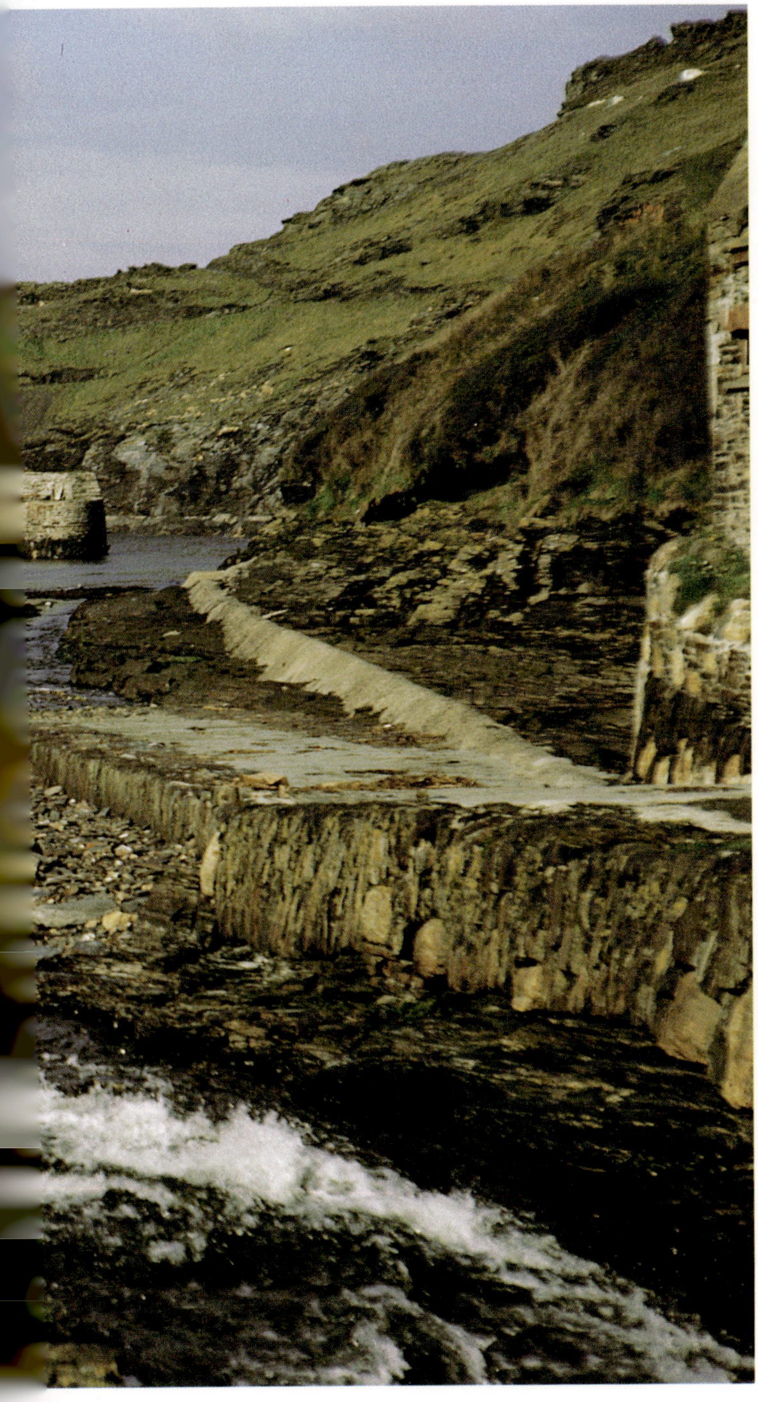

Looking out to the Atlantic

From Boscastle's sea-wall, there is something about the view that is reminiscent of the Norwegian fjords, though on a smaller scale. It is a marvellous refuge in a storm.

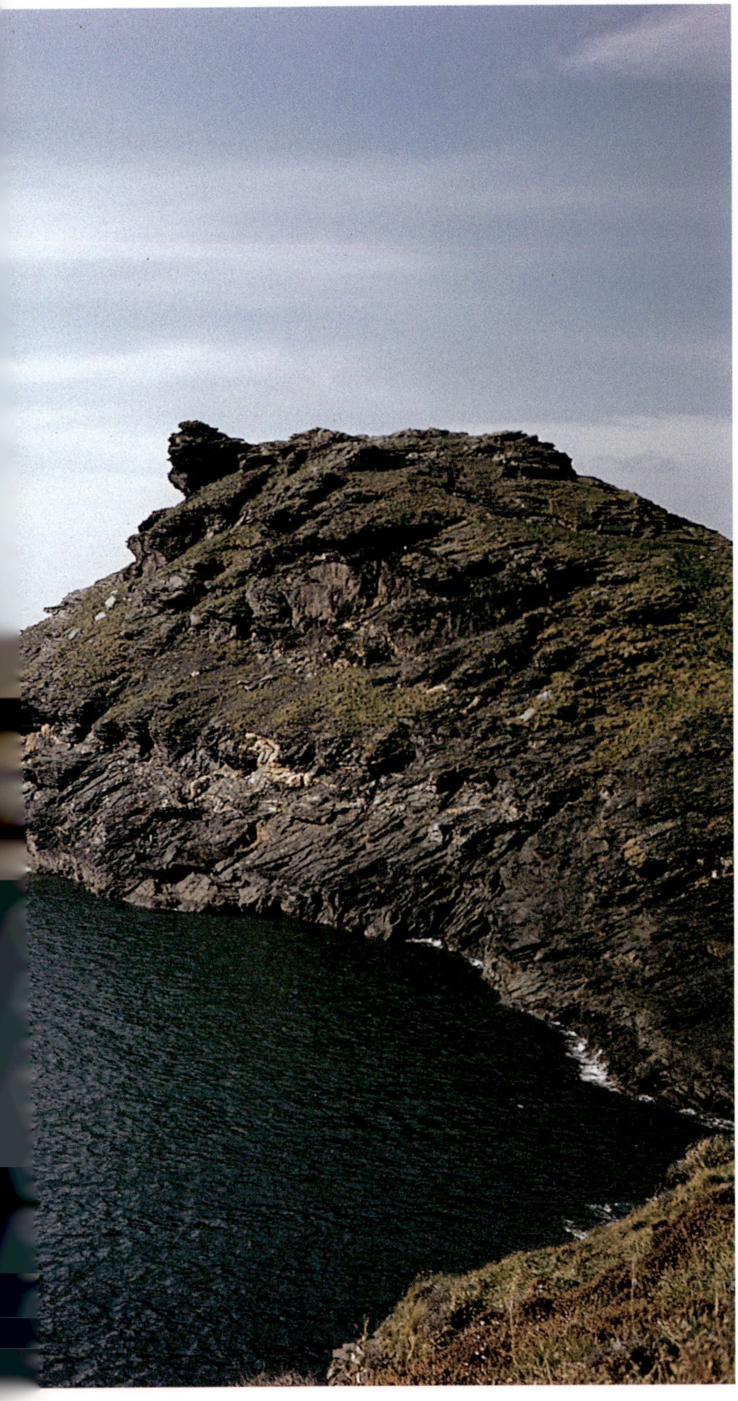

Lobster pots at Bude

Bude is one of North Cornwall's most bracing resorts, for in a gale the Atlantic rises higher here than elsewhere. Its striated cliffs, twisting and tilting in all directions, are another splendid subject for the photographer.

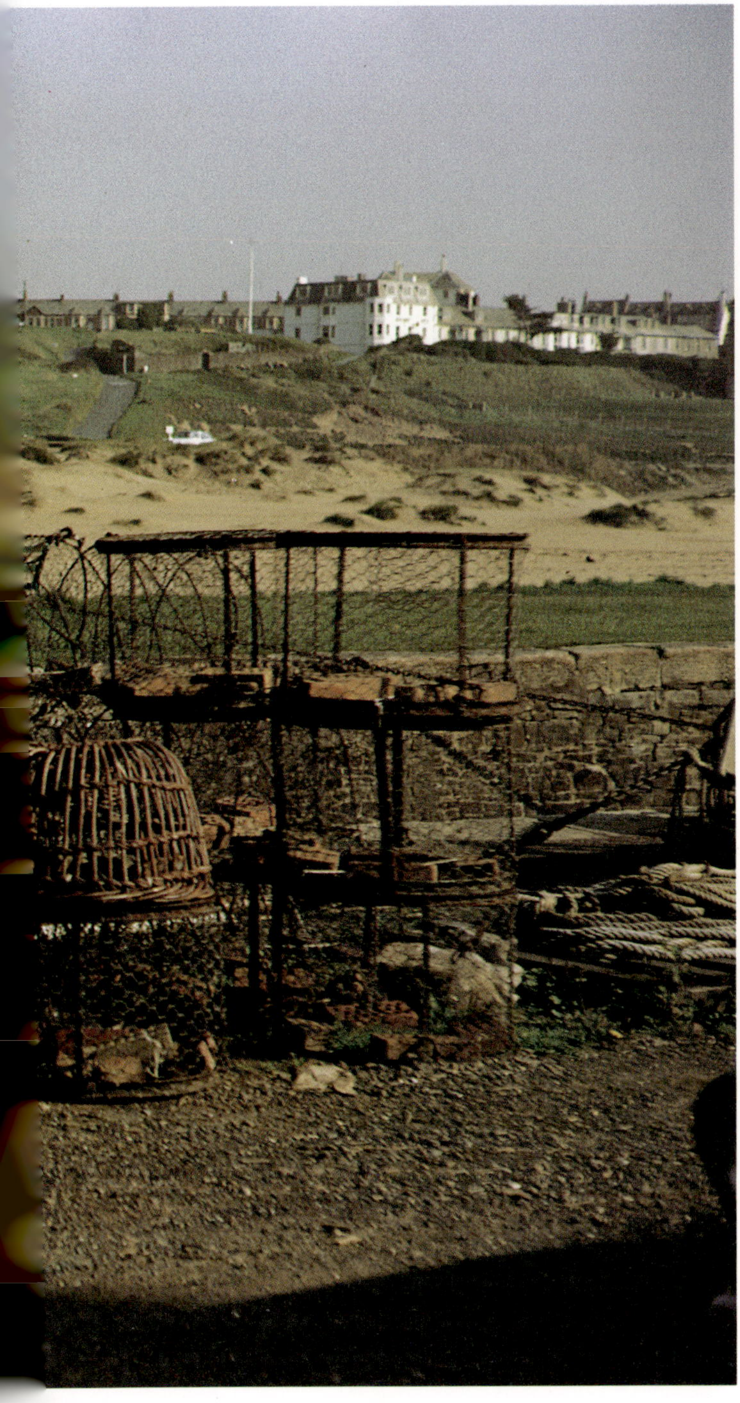

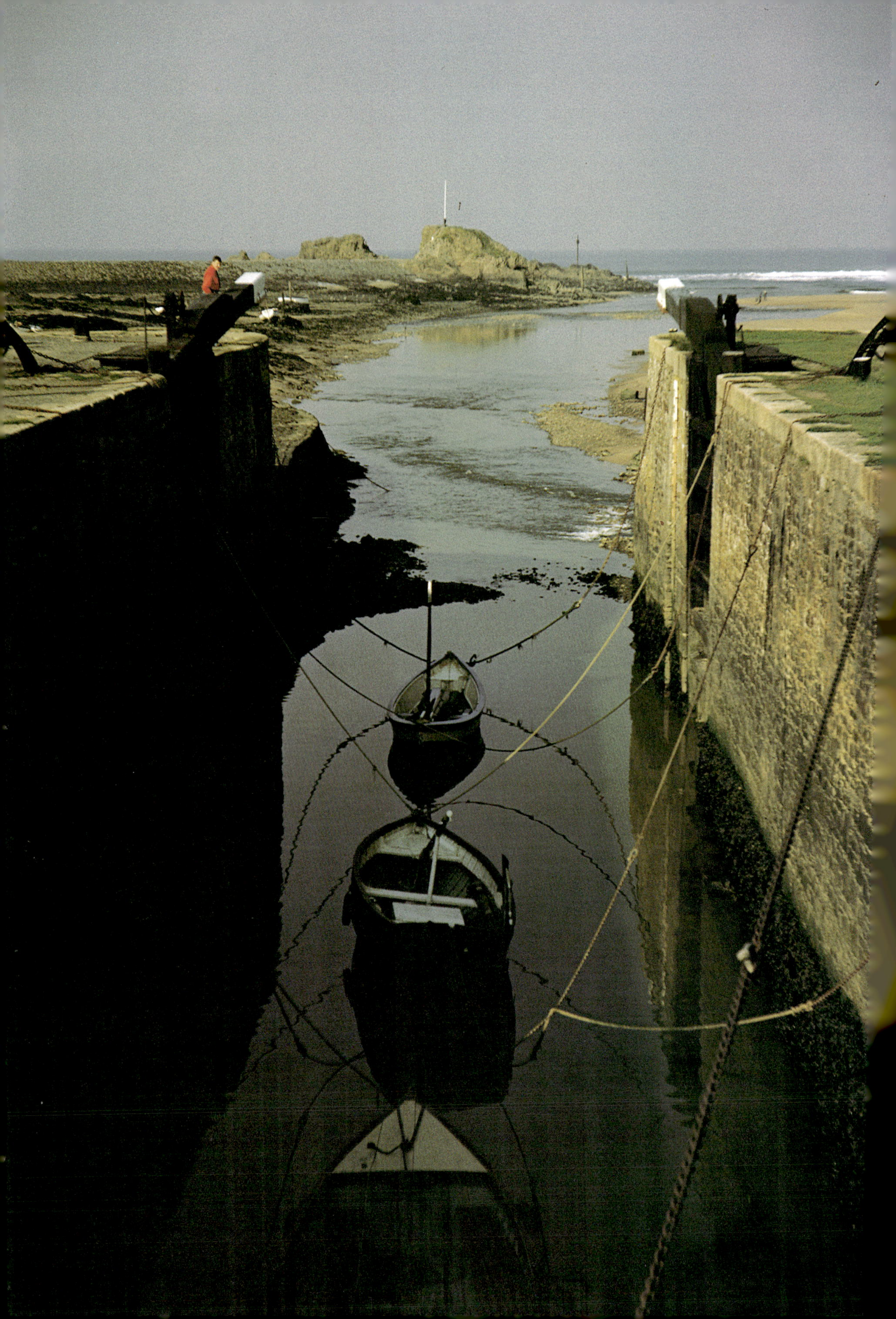

Bude Canal

The lock gates of this now-disused waterway open right on to the sea.

The view from Hartland Quay

We are back in Devon again – North Devon, this time, where the sheerness and height of the magnificent cliffs are breathtaking.

Clovelly

(overleaf)

The steep, cobbled, stepped street of this North Devon village is famous. Cars cannot use it – in earlier times people travelled up and down it by donkey, but visitors must now go on foot.

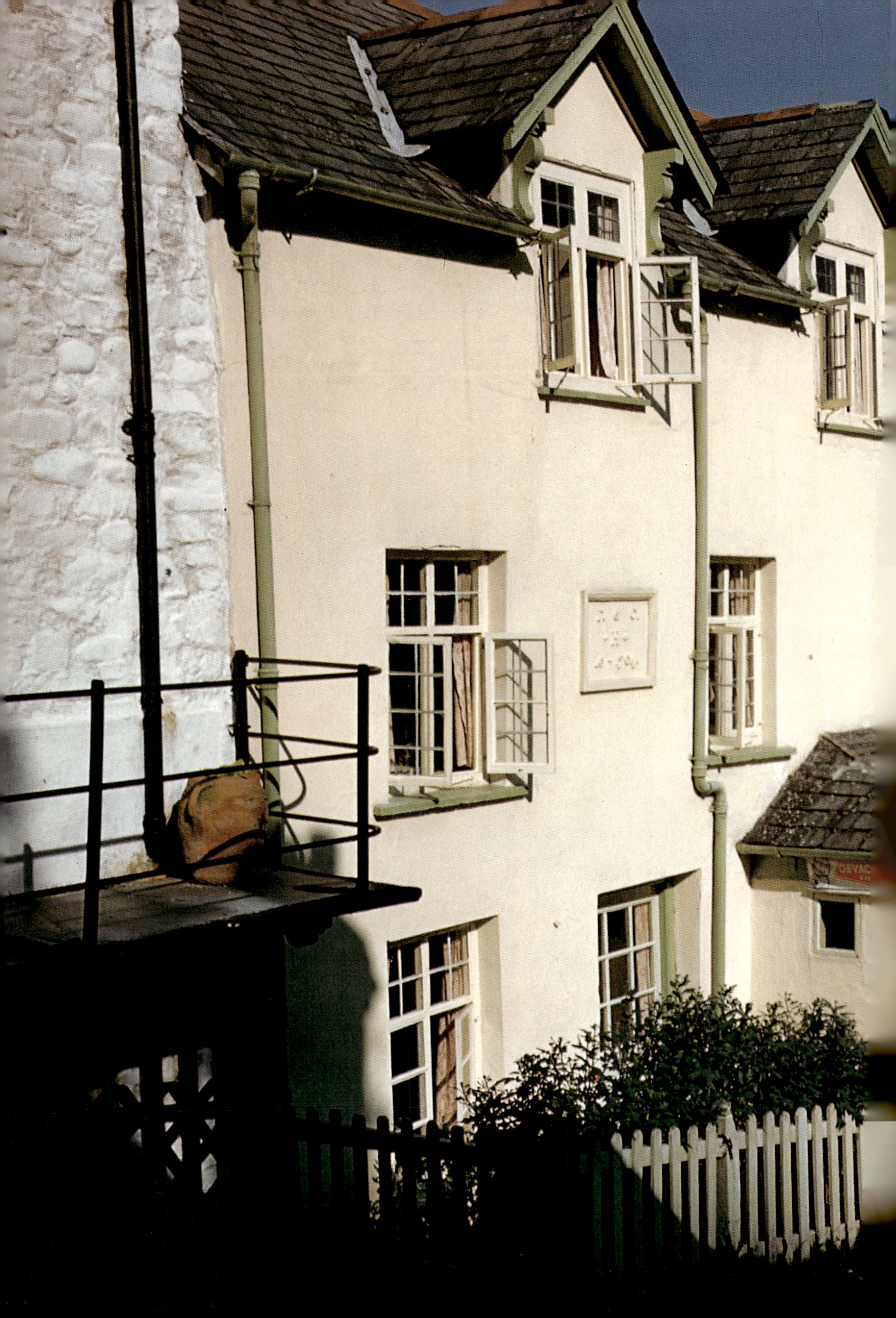

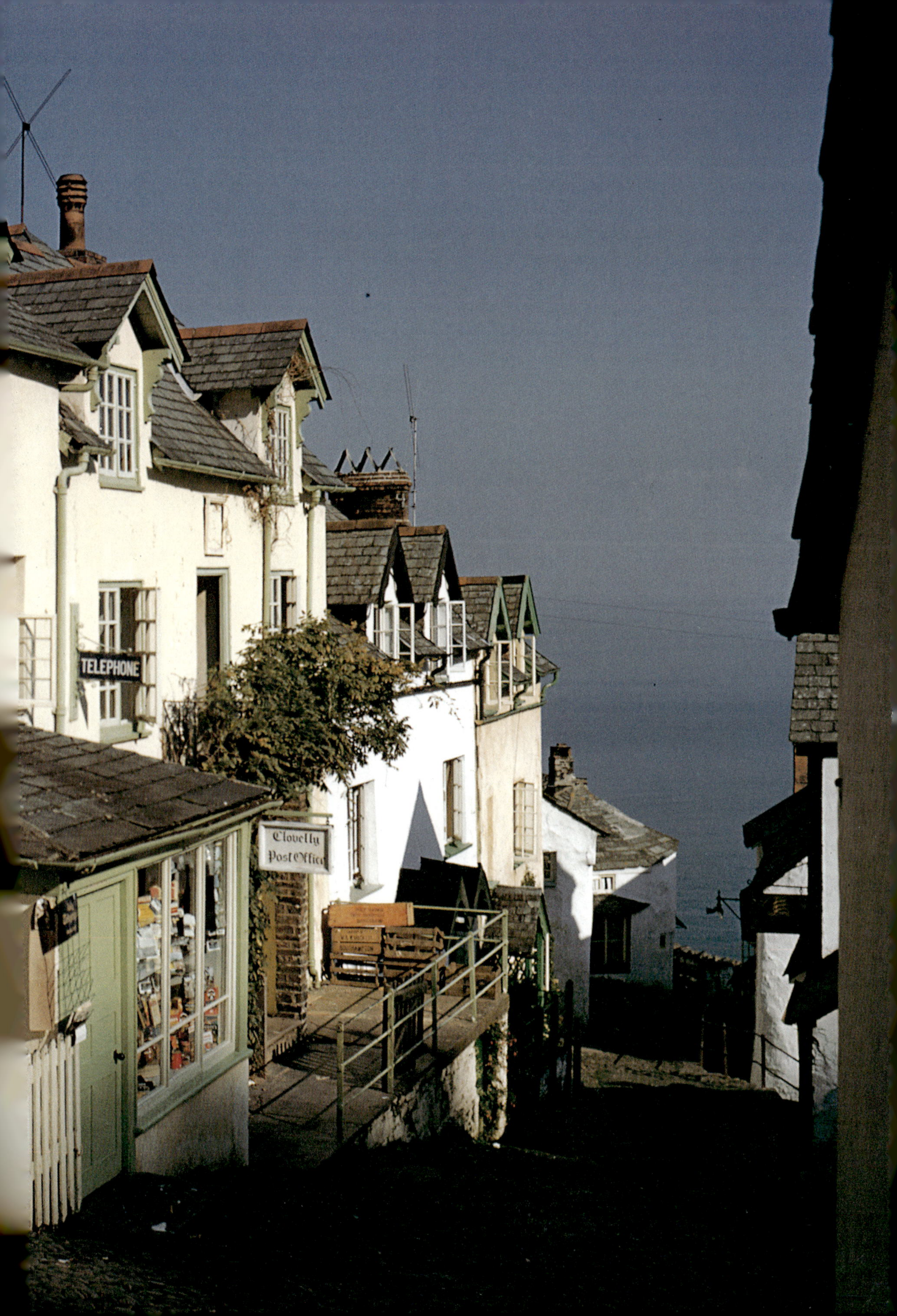
TELEPHONE
Clovelly
Post Office

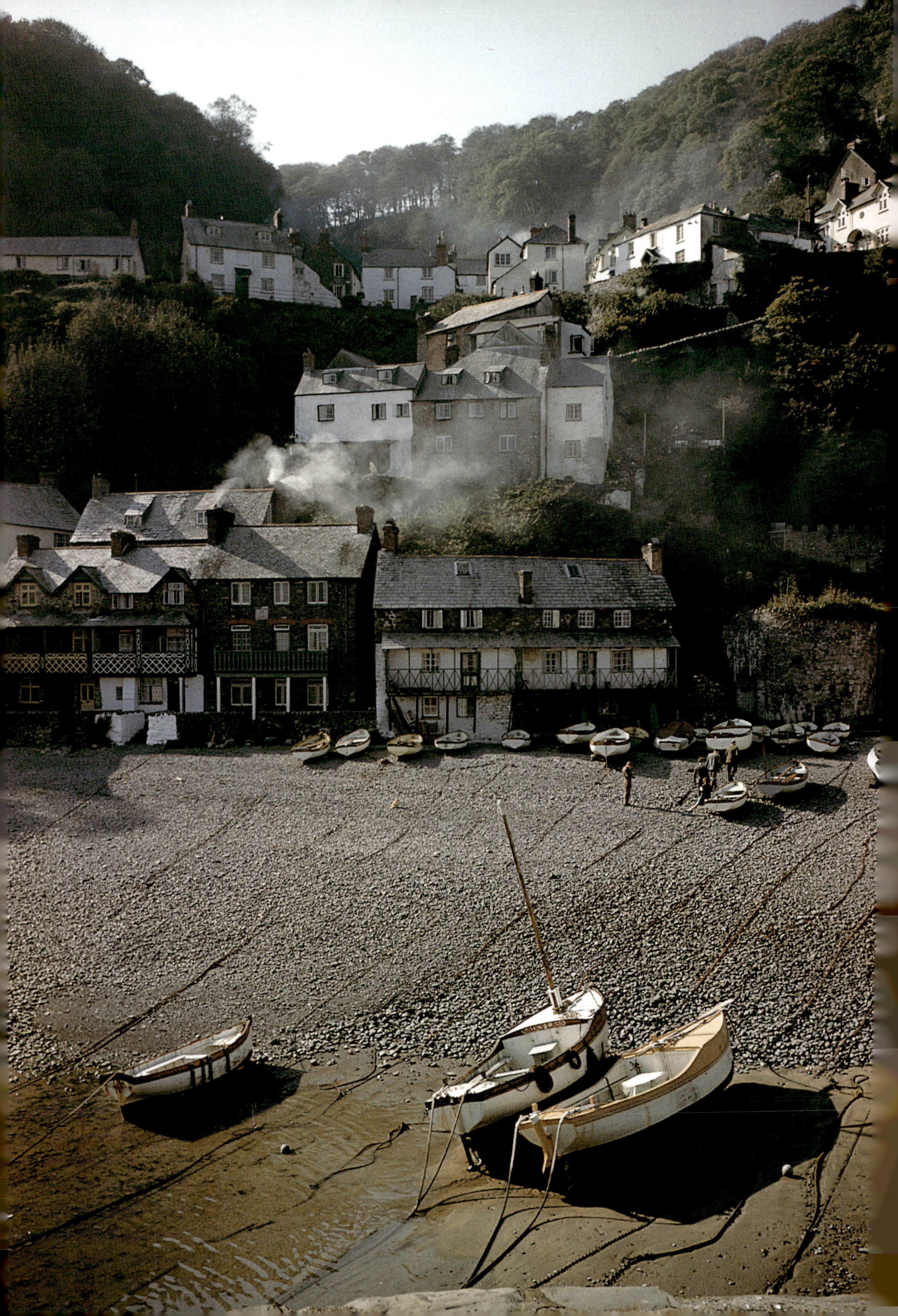

Clovelly harbour

The tranquil little pebble beach with its fishing boats and unique overhanging village behind, is possibly the most popular photographic subject in the county.

Bideford Bridge
(overleaf)

Bideford, one of the prettiest towns in North Devon, lies on the west bank of the River Torridge, which is spanned by a 24-arched stone bridge leading to East-by-the-water, seen in this picture. The first bridge on this site was probably built in the thirteenth century, but this one dates substantially from the fifteenth. On the right can be seen the old Royal Hotel, once a rich merchant's house, where Charles Kingsley is said to have written *Westward Ho!*

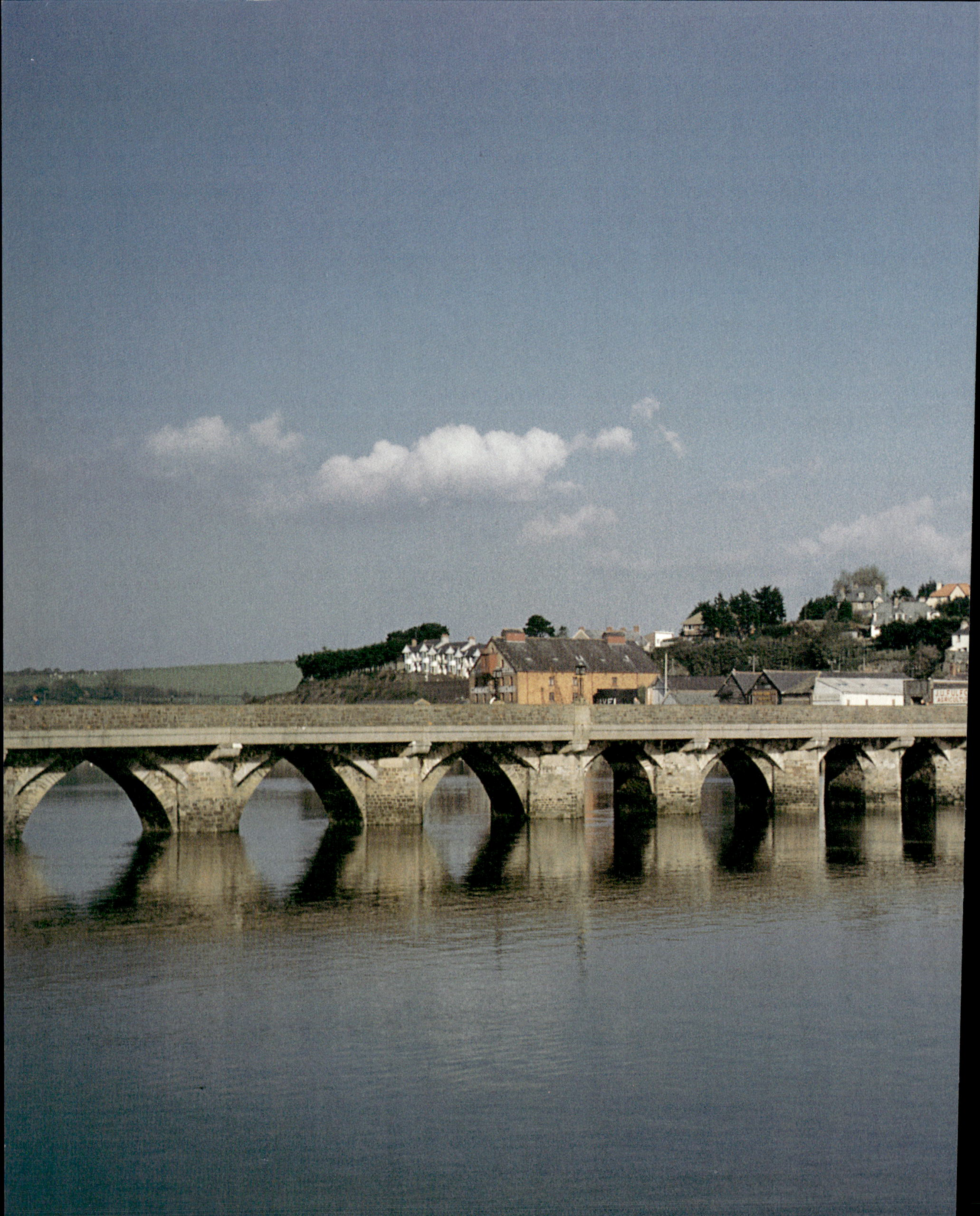

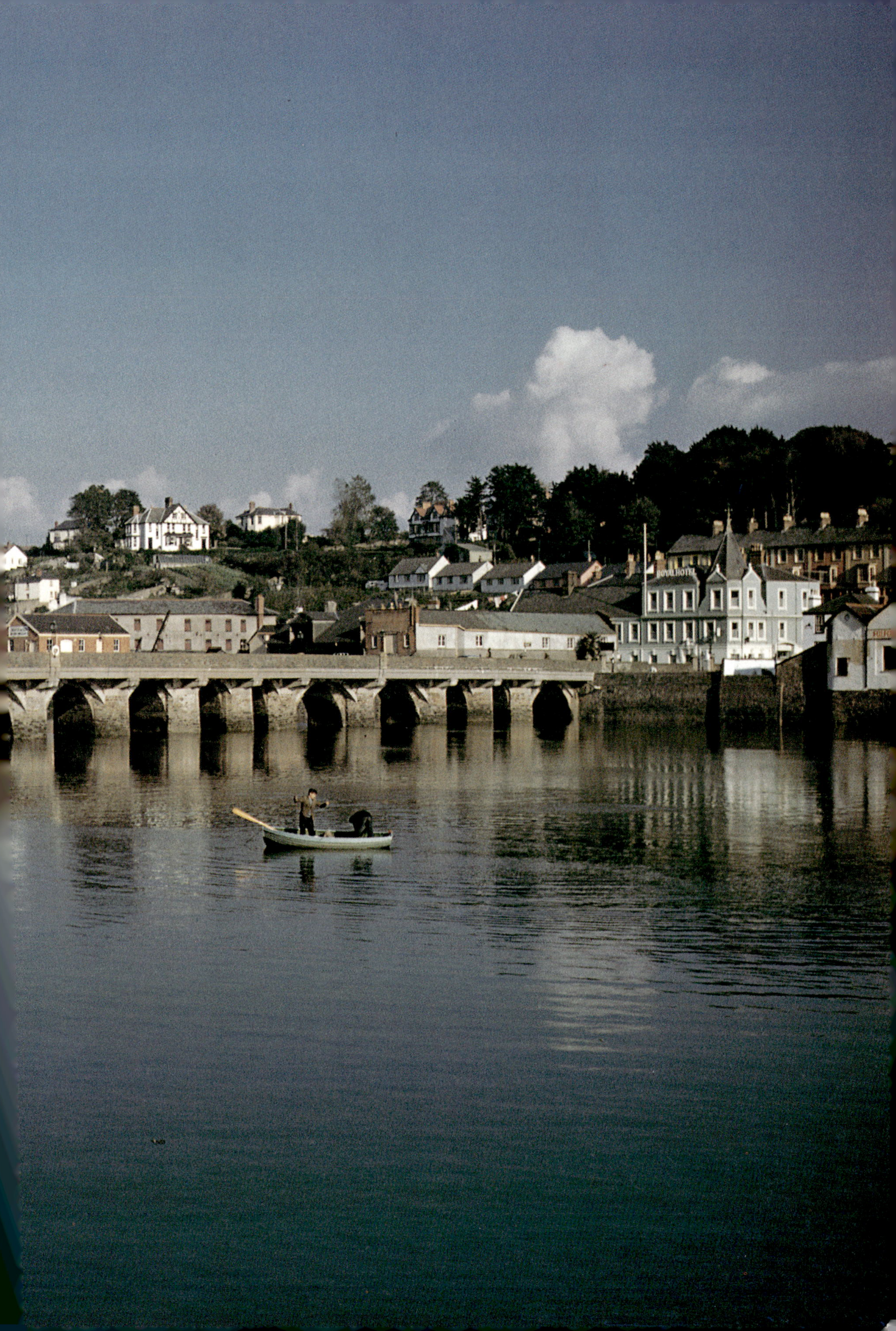
ROYAL HOTEL

The Valley of the Rocks

This rocky curve, backed by the blue sea, is within easy walking distance along the cliffs from Lynton – the town at the top of the cliffs linked to Lynmouth at the bottom (devastated by a flood in 1952) by a cliff railway.

Wells Cathedral

(overleaf)

When leaving the West Country with its natural scenic splendours, visitors should pass through Somerset to admire this wonderful man-made masterpiece, whose three south-facing towers are so superbly decorated.

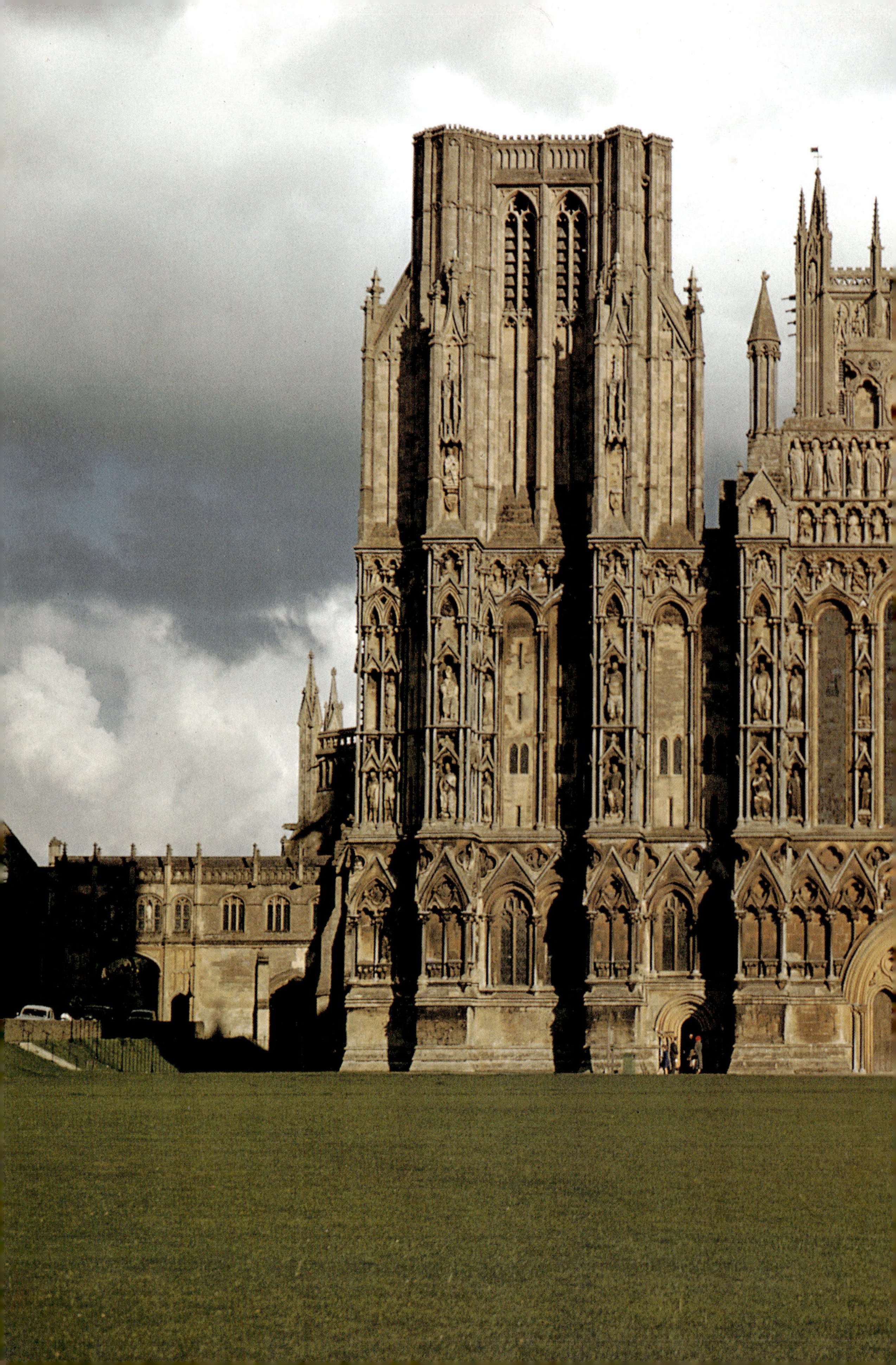

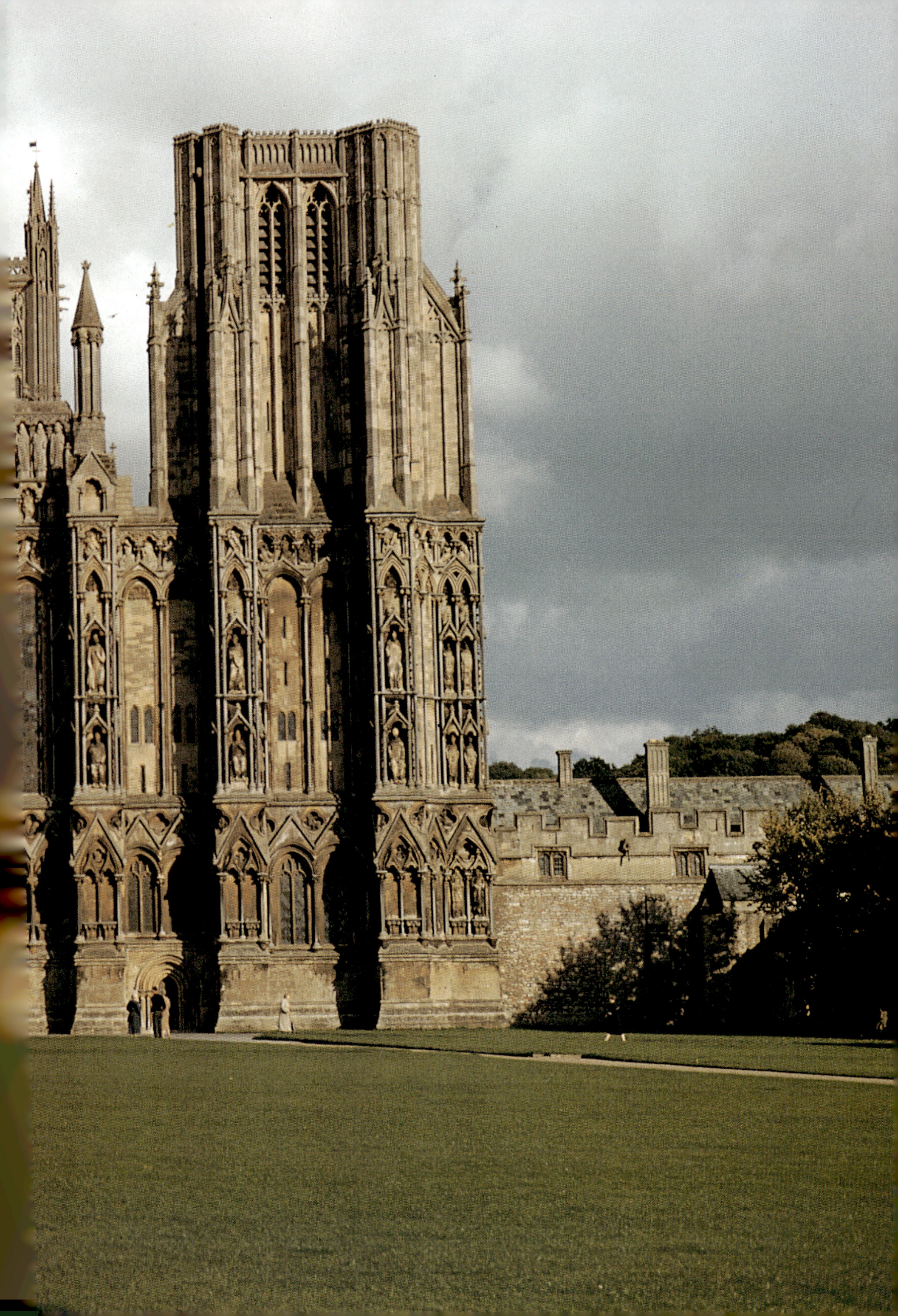